Praise For

Finding Joy Beyond Cl.
Inspiring Stories to Guide You to a Fulfilling Life

'With a combination of professional assuredness and survivor's empathy, Lesley Pyne offers reassurance and inspiration to women facing a life without children. Through the honest telling of her story, and the stories of other childless-not-by-choice women, Lesley guides readers through the challenges of making peace with an unanticipated life path, and offers exercises and suggestions to inspire transformation. Like a trusted friend, this book dishes up frank advice with a healthy dose of compassion.'

— Lisa Manterfield, author of
Life Without Baby: Surviving and Thriving
When Motherhood Doesn't Happen

'There's nothing quite so daunting as personal reinvention in the wake of trauma and loss. In sharing her story and the learnings of others who patched themselves up the hard way, Lesley Pyne gently guides readers down a path to discover and embrace one's true self.'

— Pamela Mahoney Tsigdinos,
author of Silent Sorority

'Lesley's work has been an inspiration to me, and I know this book will help many people find new purpose and passion for their life without the children they always dreamed of having.'

— Jessica Hepburn, author of
The Pursuit of Motherhood and 21 Miles:
Swimming in Search of the Meaning of Motherhood

'When I gave up on having a longed for child I never ever imagined that anything good could come from it, never. I certainly didn't believe that not getting what I wanted most could lead to self-love, self-compassion, a change in how I would love and care for myself, new meaning, a greater awareness of my values, and so much more (I was wrong). The notion that I could be happy without the longed for child seemed laughable on that day when the reality of my childlessness moved from a temporary state to a permanent one.

If you are suffering the despair of childlessness, it may seem like finding joy is unlikely; however, please don't be so sure—dare to read Lesley Pyne's book, Finding Joy Beyond Childlessness. It will offer not just hope, but a whole lot of wisdom, guidance, courage, compassion, understanding, and a tangible road map to finding your unique joy.

Lesley dares greatly in Finding Joy Beyond Childlessness; she, the brave and beautiful butterfly that she is, tells us her very personal story of being childless not by choice and how she emerged from a cocoon of despair and how exactly she got from despair to emergence.

As a therapist it can be a challenge to feel like I am reading anything new in a self-help book, a bit jaded I suppose—however, in reading Finding Joy Beyond Childlessness, I found myself wishing that I had it to turn to when I needed it most.

All these years later, well emerged from my own pain cocoon, I still learned much in Lesley's book about how the childlessness wound lives on in me, and I was reminded of my tendency to personalize my infertility story ('this just happened to me', which clearly isn't the case, which Lesley well illustrated) and how that very story exacerbated the narrative of me as a victim.

Thank you, Lesley, for this success of a book and for all the resources you've provided in it for myself and others who share this unique journey.

There is a path out of the pain of childlessness and Lesley does a brilliant job of leading the way out for those still suffering. If you are dealing with the despair of childlessness, read this book, answer the questions she lovingly and wisely asks, and soon the chrysalis of pain will lead to growth and emergence of an unexpected joy.'

— Tracey Cleantis, M.A., LMFT.
author of The Next Happy: Let Go of the Life You Planned and Find a New Way Forward, and An Invitation to Self-Care: Why Learning to Nurture Yourself Is the Key to the Life You've Always Wanted, 7 Principles for Abundant Living

Finding Joy Beyond Childlessness

Inspiring Stories to Guide You to a Fulfilling Life

Lesley Pyne

Make Your Mark Global Publishing, Ltd
USA & Monaco

MAKE YOUR MARK GLOBAL

MAKE YOUR MARK GLOBAL PUBLISHING, LTD
USA & Monaco
Time to Rise © 2018 Lesley Pyne
Published by Make Your Mark Global Publishing, LTD

Book cover design: Andrea Danon & Stefan Komljenović of Art Biro Network
Editor: Carol Taylor of Brown Sugar Books

Library of Congress Cataloging-in-Publication Data
Library of Congress Control Number: 2018943809
Finding Joy Beyond Childlessness
Publisher: Make Your Mark Global, LTD
Fernley, Nevada
p.304
Paperback ISBN 978-0-9992579-2-0
Subjects: Psychology
Summary: In Finding Joy Beyond Childlessness, Lesley Pyne uses her life experience as a childless woman, the experiences of other childless women from all over the world—who she calls her storytellers, and her skills as a coach and NLP Master Practitioner to gently guide readers through their pain to help them get to the other side to find their joy.
Printed in the USA & UK

MAKE YOUR MARK GLOBAL PUBLISHING, LTD
USA & Monaco
For information on bulk purchase orders of this book or to book Dr. Andrea or any of the authors in this book to speak at your event or on your program, call +1 707 776-6310 or send an email to
Andrea@MakeYourMarkGlobal.com

Dedication

To Melanie, Jill, Lisa, Eleanor, Ann, Dulcie, and Jill, for always being there and keeping me grounded.

To Judy because without your tenacity and determination in keeping MTL going none of this would have happened.

And to Emma, for gently leading me home to me.

Contents

Foreword

In 2011 I sat alone in front of my computer writing something for Gateway Women, a new blog I'd just started. In that piece of writing, I described my isolation, my fear, and my loneliness about being childless not by choice. I'd been grieving my childlessness for a couple of years at that point (although I didn't yet know it was grief) and I was desperate for someone (anyone!) to hear how I felt – and to do so without closing me down with some version of a miracle baby story. However, I'd given up hope that it would happen, either personally or professionally. I'd looked for books, groups, and websites, but had found nothing. So, I pressed publish on that first blog, and my life changed. I found that all around the world there were others like me who were feeling the same way. My healing began. And here I am, seven years later writing the foreword for Lesley's book – another sister who has walked her version of that same path.

One of the quotes from my work that often gets shared is this: 'The room called childlessness has many doors.' And so it is with Lesley and I, who have each arrived here via very different routes. Lesley's has involved trying and failing to conceive within her marriage followed by failed infertility treatments. She and her husband found solace and support together through the support group for couples offered by More To Life, and their life and their marriage have survived their childlessness. For me, an early abortion was followed by later 'unexplained infertility' in my marriage, which broke down under that and other strains, followed by a few years of desperate Internet dating hoping to meet someone and 'do

IVF', before a shocking slide into the abyss of grief as a single and childless woman in my mid-forties. However, what Lesley and I have both discovered in our work of supporting other childless women to heal is this: however different our stories are, the feelings we share are overwhelmingly similar.

Some of the feelings that childless women experience must be some of the hardest ones for human beings to deal with, and can include: loss, grief, depression, suicidal urges, worthlessness, futility, shame, guilt, envy, jealousy, sadness, regret, fear, anger, and an existential meaninglessness that can feel like it's going to swallow us whole. And yet, whilst we grapple with this profound dark night of the soul (many of us with no prior experience with the depth of sorrow that the human heart and mind is capable of) the response we may often receive from others might be that somehow we are 'lucky' that we get to 'sleep in at the weekends' or 'travel' and that really, 'kids aren't all they're cracked up to be'. Faced with the biggest crisis of meaning of our lives, we're told that it's really time to 'stop moping'. Unable to face the world, to be around family members or to cope with others' happiness because of the piercing physical and emotional pain it causes, we're accused of 'self-indulgence'. Yet our pain is bitingly real, and the longer we try to put a brave face on it because that's what others keep telling us to do, all that happens is that our grief gets pushed deeper and deeper inside us until it pierces our very soul. With nowhere to go, nowhere to be heard, it eats us alive from the inside out.

If you've picked up this book, you know this pain and you're desperate for some relief. You've probably already tried a few other things. Maybe you've done your best to stuff it down and ignore it but have seen it leak out and make a nasty mess in your family, your friendships, your romantic life, and at work. Maybe you've thrown yourself headlong into a new project and have exhausted yourself with overwork, or have begun to worry yourself and others with your less socially acceptable addictive behaviors like overeating or drinking too much. Maybe you've been to the doctor, to therapists and counsellors but have not felt that they've understood the depth or the lifelong ramifications of your loss. Perhaps they have hinted or suggested that you should 'count your blessings' or 'be more mindful' (this appears to be the modern way to say 'suck it up'!) Perhaps, if you are a woman of faith, you've taken your sadness to your God and your faith community, but found no solace there either as mothers, baby on hip, tell you that your childlessness is 'God's will' and that 'He has other plans for you'. Maybe you've tried antidepressants, run marathons, changed jobs, partners, countries, and haircuts but are still left with an overwhelming sense of emptiness in your heart and, no matter how sorted you appear on the outside, at 3am, the hour of the wolf, you're awake, feeling hollowed out and wondering if you will ever feel whole again.

So, here you are. Another book. Another hope that *maybe* this one will help. Really? After all you've been through? And the answer is both yes and no.

No – because ultimately no book, no matter how brilliant it is, is going to get you to where you need to go; it can only ever be a guide to the inner journey you must make, and only you can make that journey. Yes – because this book is an excellent guide to that path, written by one who has walked it, lived it, and who tells the truth about how hard it is and where the dragons are. If you follow it, you will find some relief, gain much wisdom, and feel a whole lot less alone. It's not going to fix your life, because the human condition is not fixable, only loveable. But it will give you insights, tools, and techniques to live the life that has chosen you rather than to endure it. Perhaps you were hoping for more of a miracle than that, but having found my own way to live the life unexpected, I can assure you that it will be miracle enough.

Lesley's voice and book are very different to mine as she and I are very different women. She was born and brought up in the North of England which, for those of you who aren't British, doesn't have a culture of 'self-help', or not at least the kind that you find in bookshops – it's more one of stoic self-resilience, self-reliance, and self-abnegation; what our American sisters would call 'grit'. Perhaps it's one of the last bastions of the 'stiff upper lip' for which Brits are still famed for around the world! As a 'softie Southerner' (as I would be referred to by native Northerners), I have really come to appreciate through the autobiographical elements of Lesley's story how much more powerfully the social shame of childlessness can fester into a deep sense of personal failure when we don't feel we're 'allowed' to suffer; when our cultural conditioning instructs us that the best way to overcome suffering is to 'toughen up'. So I guess it's no surprise then how powerfully the work of Brené Brown impacted Lesley – another 'tough love' native, this time a Texan, and one who learned that vulnerability is the key to creativity and joy, and then shared her own vulnerability in a TED talk that went viral. Brené meet

Lesley, your sister from another mother! For women who are wary of 'self-help' as being a little bit suspect, Lesley's voice, background, and personal journey towards reuniting her body and mind in the service of her healing from childlessness will ring very true. And it is true. I first met Lesley many years ago and the transformation she describes from being in her head to in her heart is one I have seen. In those early days, my impression was that she wore her body like armour and my friendly overtures were met by a chill wariness. These days, as you're about to read, that carapace has softened to reveal a tenderness of heart and vulnerability that not only seeks connection, but also welcomes it, embraces it, values it.

The healing journey that Lesley is about to take you on – from your head to your heart, from your mind to your body – is one that many of us need to make, not just once, but again and again in our lives. It's one I've had to make too, and it's a shero's journey in the Joseph Campbell mould. Because the process of transformation isn't comfortable, pretty, convenient, or fun. It's one that we humans resist fiercely because it means letting go of what we know in order to become a version of ourselves we haven't met yet. It's about surrendering control and letting go in order to step into a new version of ourselves. Those are easy words to write; they are incredibly hard to do. One of the things I really appreciate about this book is that Lesley doesn't sugarcoat it. She's not one for, 'If you build it, they will come' or any other kind of magical thinking, which would be an anathema to her pragmatic Northern roots. Tell it how it is and do so with compassion is more her style. It's immensely reassuring and relatable.

The metaphor of the butterfly is one that's often used to describe the process of transformation, usually illustrated by a lovely photograph. The focus is nearly always on the end stage, the beautiful butterfly – less so on the actual process of transformation, of the caterpillar happily munching on a leaf without a care in the world when suddenly its body starts turning to mush and before long it finds itself in a prison-like cocoon with no idea how it got there or what awaits it. In this book, Lesley quotes one of my favorite compassionate tough love writers, Maya Angelou in that, 'We delight in the beauty of the butterfly, but rarely admit the changes it has gone through to achieve that beauty'. This book is for those in the cocoon, wondering what the hell happened and perhaps not even aiming as high as becoming a butterfly – right now they just want to get out of that damn cocoon!

If that's you, *welcome*. You're not alone in your cocoon, Lesley is going to climb in there with you and share her own instructions for release, as well as the stories of many other women, myself included, who've been where you're at right now and have found their way out. The threads of the cocoon were woven slightly differently for each of us, so the route out is slightly different for each of us too. But you are not alone anymore. Your own transformation is about to begin. And out here in the sunshine, your childless sisters await you, as does the rest of your life.

Jody Day, Founder of Gateway Women
and author of *Living the Life Unexpected:
12 Weeks to Your Plan B for a Meaningful and
Fulfilling Future Without Children*

Preface

.... nothing is as uncomfortable, dangerous and hurtful as believing that I'm standing on the outside of my life looking in and wondering what it would be like if I had the courage to show up and let myself be seen.

Brené Brown, from Daring Greatly: How the Courage to Be Vulnerable Transforms the Way We Live, Love, Parent and Lead

When I first read these words in January 2013 they absolutely jolted me to the core as I realised how perfectly they described my life. I was standing on the outside, hiding my true self. And it hurt. A lot.

It's taken me five years, losing my dad, a lot of courage, and doing the work of each chapter in this book to say confidently that I am now fully showing up in my life.

I can truly say that I am at peace with my past; for the first time in my life, I know who I am and I'm living a life I absolutely love.

I'm guessing you feel those words hurting you to the core, too.

If they do, this book is for you. It's for you if you wanted to be a mother and for some reason it didn't happen. You're feeling devastated, sad, angry, disappointed, (I could go on...) and mostly...you're hiding your true self from the world. And it hurts. A lot.

I have good news.

Other women have walked this path, and they are now showing up in the world as themselves and living a fulfilling life without the children they desperately wanted.

I have more good news.

You *can* do this. I believe this passionately, but you don't have to believe me just yet. On my website I publish what I've called Inspirational Stories, stories of real childless women who have stood where you're standing now, hiding themselves, but are now showing up happily in their life. I realised that there were some common things they did to get through it, and together we will dig into these subjects. Using their stories, my own experience and teachings, I will show you how you can stop hiding and show up in the world as yourself.

I also have bad news.

No one is coming to save you. Only you can do the work and it might not be easy. I'd love to be able to wave a magic wand and make it all better, but we both know that's not how life works. By now you'll have worked out that time on its own isn't the great healer that it's said to be. Time will pass anyway, so I invite you to use some of your time to read on and be open to the possibility that I (and the ladies who share their stories here) might be able to help you.

Before you start, here's my story in brief, you'll read more of it in each chapter.

My Story: Keeping Everything In A Box

I always assumed that one day I'd be a mother. It never crossed my mind that I wouldn't. My husband Roger and I spent the first three years of our marriage enjoying being together. As far as we knew, there was no rush to try for children; we had plenty of time. Then when I was 35 we decided to try. If I'd known then how fast my fertility was falling, maybe our lives would have been different.

After a few months nothing happened so we saw the doctor and the next thing we knew we were referred for IVF. Over the next three years we went through six unsuccessful rounds, stopping when I was 40.

We knew we needed to draw a line in the sand but it was incredibly hard. We were never offered support or help of any kind and felt as if we were the only people in the world who couldn't have children. Only our parents knew and most of our friends had children so talking to them felt impossible.

My 40th birthday was a low point. I felt completely alone; I didn't know who I was or my place in the world. I felt like a caterpillar in a cocoon that didn't know what sort of butterfly it was going to become. I know now that I was grieving, but I didn't know then. I just assumed I was sad. I didn't know how to feel, so on the outside I projected the Lesley who was ambivalent about children, the Lesley who was tough and strong.

We hibernated for about a year and didn't see friends because we couldn't cope with hearing about and seeing their children. Then we joined More To Life (MTL is the part of Fertility Network UK, dedicated to those who are childless) and met some couples who have become our closest friends.

I slowly started to get my life back together, although I still felt sad. Then my life fell apart again when Roger's dad died, followed a few months later by my mum.

Now I knew I was grieving and did what I'd always done, which was to box it away. And there it stayed. I just carried on and sadness became my new norm. I stayed in my cocoon, only emerging from time to time to meet up with childless friends.

When I was 47 I resigned from my job. I had no idea who I was and what I wanted, but I knew it wasn't this. It was a partial release, and at the same time a step back into my cocoon. I decided to train as a Neuro Linguistic Programming Master Practitioner. (NLP is the study of the language of the mind, patterns of thinking and behavior and a series of techniques and tools to assist people in changing their behaviors so they can have more of what they want and less of what they don't want.) Following this I set up a coaching business to help women in midlife. I wanted to support childless women but didn't feel strong enough to do it because it meant being open about my story and myself.

This was when I first read Brené's quote. It shocked me to the core and gave me the courage to reach out and work with a coach who believed in me and the difference I wanted to make in the world. She supported me in changing my business to support childless women.

I thought, *yes* now I'm showing up in my life, job done!

Not so.

In 2014 my dad died after a short illness. For a while I told myself that this was new and different grief and not linked to the past. I boxed that away as well. And there it stayed. Until it didn't. Because (as I've learned the hard way), one way or another, grief will find its way out. After struggling and resisting for a long time, I started to work with a therapist who helped me with my grief work and many other things.

Then one day in a yoga class, I heard a really strong calling to write a book. I saw myself at the publication party surrounded by close friends and those who've helped me and the book become a reality. My body was flooded with wonderful feelings as I realised how much I wanted to:

- Hold the book in my hand and

- Show other women that they can have a fulfilling life and how to achieve it.

I started to write. Now that I've finished, I realise there was something else. I believe that vision was my soul calling. First it sent me a sprained ankle to slow me down, then came a voice in my head saying 'you can't do this' and other such negativity. Luckily it also gave me permission to ask for help from the magical helpers it also sent my way. My soul was indeed calling me to do the work, to really grieve, to let go, to connect with my body, to write, to truly accept myself, to be grateful for everything and to find joy. And mostly it was calling me to fully show up in my life.

Now, having done the work I can say confidently that '*I absolutely love my life and the adventures I'm having, and I'm excited about what will happen next.*'

How can I have so much joy and happiness in my life that I could cry? After all I've been through, coming to terms with being childless and losing both parents, how on earth can I be this happy?

If you read on, you'll find out and learn how you can have this too.

Childless or Childfree?

I use the term childless here. To be honest I hate it and it's not a label I claim. It seems bizarre to define ourselves by something we don't have, but to date I haven't found anything better and it's what many people search for online, so I use it with reluctance.

Some say that in time you get to a place where you call yourself childfree. I don't. To me childfree describes those who made a conscious choice not to have children. Childless describes those of us who wanted to be a mother and when it didn't happen, struggled to come to terms with our life. You thought that motherhood was your path, and now that it's not going to happen you don't know who you are in the world.

Becoming The Beautiful Butterfly That's Inside You

I believe this journey of ours is similar to the transformation a caterpillar goes through to become a beautiful butterfly. I've written the book in three acts that are loosely based on this process.

Act One – Call To Life

I've called this act a call to life, because to me that's what it is, a call to a full and authentic life; to become the beautiful butterfly that's hidden inside you. You can stay a caterpillar for as long as you like but the call will keep coming until you answer it. For many years I refused to answer the call to grieve and in the end it was ringing so loudly that I was forced to. I'm glad I did.

Act One is also about getting ready for what comes next. To that end, you'll read why story is important and I'll teach you some tools to help you on your way. I'll also introduce you to our storytellers, 19 brave and inspiring women who have shared their story so you might learn and take inspiration from them.

You'll also hear from the first of several 'experts'. You can read in the Resources section what makes them an expert.

Act Two – Finding Your Wings

Here is where you do the work. Like the caterpillar in the cocoon, this is where you go through the process of transformation into a butterfly. Also like a caterpillar, you will gradually shed the skin of your old life and the stories that were keeping you stuck.

In each chapter I explore something that a number of the storytellers did to help them through. Some of these themes will resonate with you, and some won't. That's okay. To quote Joseph Campbell: *'If you can see your path laid out in front of you step by step, you know it's not your path. Your own path you make with every step you take. That's why it's your path'.*

You won't be travelling alone. In addition to the stories, I've included some theory, and my own experience.

As you step in here you'll let go of the old story and it will take time before you start to tell a new one. You might feel like you're falling, as things you thought you knew and who you thought you were drop away. It will be uncomfortable, and as this saying by Baal Shem Tov goes, *'let me fall if I must. The one I will become will catch me'*.

I'm afraid it's not going to be easy; there's a lot going on in the cocoon. If you were to open a cocoon in the middle of transformation, a sort of caterpillar soup would ooze out. In this soup are something called 'imaginal discs' which contain the coded instructions to make the butterfly. So it is with you, deep inside you, are the instructions for your particular butterfly, and you might have to dig deep to find and understand them. In case you haven't already worked it out; to get to the happy ending you will have to change yourself. I will show you how.

Act Three – Learning to Fly

I believe it's impossible to go through the challenge of infertility and not be changed by the process. Here you will read how the storytellers created meaning in their lives and how they now embrace the gifts that a childless life brings.

After going through Act Two, you will discover what sort of beautiful butterfly you really are and be ready to gently unfurl your wings and learn to fly. You will start to move forward and write a new story of your life.

- You are now comfortable in your own skin.

- You're happy to speak about your life should you wish to do so.

- You have the courage to be authentically you and embrace your life as it is today.

Pause for a moment and imagine how relieved and excited you'll feel, knowing that you have the confidence that comes from permanently leaving the pain behind and are now ready for the future.

Are you ready to join me?

If you're ready to join me and achieve that fulfilling life, I thank you for trusting me.

If you're not yet sure that's okay too, you never have to answer the call. But know that it won't stop, and the longer you ignore it, the louder it will be and the harder the journey will become. You can stay as a caterpillar forever, but wouldn't it be sad to live your life never knowing who you really are and how beautiful you could be?

How To Get The Most From This Book

There are no rules and I know from experience that making one successful change emboldens you to make others, and before long you've made a lot of progress. I guess I'm saying don't aim too high to start with.

You can start reading anywhere, or read the whole book in one sitting. However, wherever you start, you'll get the most out of it if you read it slowly and consciously, working through it at your own pace.

You'll read in Chapter Ten how helpful it is to have a writing practice. Instead of waiting until you get there, I suggest you start now. Buy yourself a lovely journal, and set aside some time after reading to write about what occurs to you, and how what you've read might show up in your life.

Each chapter ends with a section called Journaling Questions which includes suggestions and questions to help you, so establishing a writing practice now will help you to dig deep into these. Some chapters have a lot of questions, please know that you don't have to answer all (or any) of them. Pick those which resonate with you. Or maybe pick the ones that you have most resistance to because that could be where your biggest growth will be.

It's also not a linear journey. You may wish to circle back and reconsider chapters and questions you missed the first time or you've already worked through. As you do this you'll realise how much you are changing and growing.

If you make one change after reading it, then this book has done its work. That's the way I work with self-help books.

The most important things are to enjoy the process and be gentle with yourself.

You can also find additional content – a workbook of the Journaling Questions, videos and interviews with the storytellers, and the visualisations I mention at www.LesleyPyne.co.uk/bookresources

Act One

Call To Life

Introduction

We delight in the beauty of the butterfly, but rarely admit the changes it has gone through to achieve that beauty.

Maya Angelou

I've read that there are two sorts of people in the world:

- Those who live a half-lived life, who don't answer (or maybe don't listen to) the call. They live small lives, and maybe always have regrets. They stay as caterpillars, never knowing what sort of butterfly they might have been.

- Then there are those who use the challenges they've been given to make changes within. They hear the voice calling and feel a longing to wake up and live more fully. They know that going forward will lead to the death of the caterpillar they are now, but the prize is to become the beautiful butterfly that's been hidden inside them.

Act One is about getting ready for what comes next so you'll start by learning why story is important. I'll then introduce you to our storytellers and you'll read how they each came to this place we call childless.

In the final chapters of Act One I'll teach you some tools to get you started and share with you the importance of having a positive mindset.

Chapter One

What Story Are You Telling?

The universe is made of stories, not atoms.

Muriel Rukeyser

There is a big difference between what happens to you and the story you tell yourself about what happened. The story you tell is key because it determines the life you have. If you tell yourself that your life has no meaning and will be miserable, then it will be. However, if you tell yourself – like the women you'll meet here – that there are gifts in the childless life, and you're prepared to do what it takes to receive them, that's what will happen.

Human brains are wired for story. Stories are patterns and our brains love patterns. Uncertainty is an incomplete pattern that the brain doesn't like so it fills in the gap, releasing the feel good neurotransmitter dopamine into your system and making you feel good. Job done.

Except it fills in the gap with a story, and over time these stories become the 'truth'. For example you may be telling yourself that because you are not able to be a mother you're broken or there's something wrong with you. Let's debunk that straight away. This is a story your brain has made up and it could become the 'truth' of who you are and how you live. This is a great example of how the story you tell yourself can come true.

Your brain never stops telling stories. Stop reading for a moment, close your eyes and listen. There will be an endless stream of thoughts, ideas, and stories emanating from it. It never stops. Your world is structured around this inner dialogue and the stories it tells. Doesn't it make sense to first notice what sort of stories it is telling and then change these to stories that help and empower you?

Stories That Imprison You

Let's dig into the idea that the story you tell yourself is determining the life you're living. To quote Mahatma Gandhi:

> *Your beliefs become your thoughts.*
> *Your thoughts become your words.*
> *Your words become your actions.*
> *Your actions become your habits.*
> *Your habits become your values.*
> *Your values become your destiny.*

I know he didn't mention story but if we replace thoughts with story, you can see how the story you tell yourself can become your destiny. Can you see how the story you tell yourself can either support you or can imprison you and keep you stuck?

Let's play for a moment. Think of an area in your life where you feel stuck or helpless. Not a ten out of ten stuck, maybe a three or four. Now pause and drop into it. What's the story you're telling yourself? Find the 'should' or 'shouldn't' that's underneath it. What is it?

Now breathe and feel with it. Wouldn't you feel great if you let it go?

Now imagine how amazing you will feel when you've let go of the story you've made up about being childless?

That's what we'll be doing.

It's not just you.

Telling yourself that 'it's just me' is the biggest story of all, and the one that keeps you isolated and alone. I've already told you that's not the case but you don't have to believe me. *Yet.*

I can't tell you how many times I thought I was the only one who was struggling with something, and how much relief I felt when someone told me that they struggled too. This is why I've included stories from women who are just like you. So you will know in your bones that you are not alone, and most importantly that you can do what they have done.

My Story: Imprisoned By Words

I started practicing yoga 18 months ago and you'll read later how much it has changed me. A few months after I started I discovered that I loved Yin Yoga most of all. Yin is different from other yoga styles. You're mostly sitting or lying down, it's meditative and you hold the asanas (seats/poses) for several minutes.

There's one asana in particular that I had massive resistance to (called Saddle) and the story I made up was: *All the other students are a decade or three younger than me, a lot thinner, and way more bendy; no one else has bolsters and, no matter how hard I try I'll never make any progress.* I was telling myself *'I can't do it'* and *'I won't try'*. I was using language of impossibility, which was keeping both my mind and body in a static, unyielding place where progress was impossible. Some other phrases I could have used were, 'it's impossible', 'I choose not to', 'I don't intend to', 'I am unable to' or 'I won't try'. And yes this was in the middle of writing – I know… I'm a slow learner.

In the safe space of my private lessons I felt comfortable being vulnerable and open and my teacher encouraged me to change the story and, surprise, surprise I opened myself up further and needed less support than ever before. I started using words like 'I *can*' do this, and '*I want*' to see how far I can go. Other words I could have used are 'I am able to', 'I choose to', 'I intend to', 'I am' or 'it's possible'.

And the result? Of course it's still a story. Before it was static and unyielding and now it's one of movement, achievement, and attainment. My body changed too. It no longer screams at me to pull back; instead, the muscles in my legs and back became more relaxed, allowing me to bend further.

A few weeks later, accompanied by many tears and laughter I achieved something I thought would take me months or even years. I met Saddle without bolster or cushions, just a couple of blankets. It was *massive,* a real breakthrough, one of those where every less than helpful belief I had about myself flew out of the window; my foundations were rocked to the core.

It changed me fundamentally; friends told me I looked lighter and more relaxed. I'm certainly more grounded and comfortable in my own skin, more sensitive to sounds, tastes and colours. Most importantly, I feel more alive than ever. All because I changed the story I was telling myself from one of *impossibility* to one of *possibility*.

You can do this too.

Much later I discover that Yin is different from other yoga, where the goal is to always be moving toward a perfect pose or asana. In Yin, the opposite is true, you allow yourself to be just where your body is, in the moment, without wishing to change it and without judgement. Over time you become at one with your body, as it is, in the present moment. You invite the possibility of also inhabiting emotions, and finding more peace and calm as they are released. Hmm, it seems like my soul knew exactly what I needed when it encouraged me to practice Yin.

If you were to attempt Saddle (and I don't recommend you do unless a yoga teacher is on hand), you would sit either on your heels, with the feet under the buttocks or sit between your heels. Then you would lower your torso back so ultimately you are lying to the floor. I can hear you saying 'ouch.' It's an intense stretch of the hip flexors, quads, knees and (for me) ankles, and also a deep back compression. Initially I needed the support of two bolsters and now usually reach the floor. You can see an image of me in Saddle in the resources section of my website.

Denying Your Story

In this quote, Brené Brown encapsulates my feelings about story and the path I encourage you to take.

When you deny your story, it owns you.
When you own your story, you get to write your own brave ending.
When you deny your pain, it owns you.
When you own your pain, it sets you free.

Let's unpack it.

Let me guess, your friends don't know *why* you don't have children.

When you were trying for children you kept everything secret and now it feels too difficult to tell others the truth of your life. It's become a habit that's hard to change and, like all secrets, it's become toxic.

I believe this is what Brené means when she talks about denying your story. When you deny it, it owns you and you do everything you can to avoid telling it. Two things happen. The more you keep it to yourself, the harder it is to be honest and open, and the alternative story that you tell becomes the 'truth' and you move away from your authentic or true self.

You also become someone who pretends to be different from who they are, and you don't need me to tell you how incredibly hard it is to not be your authentic self.

What Does Owning Your Story Mean?

This means firstly being honest with *yourself* about the reality of your life, accepting that you're childless. And yes, I understand that this is a *big* thing. But think about it for a moment, if you continue to deny this truth, how are you ever going to be happy? I also know this isn't a quick fix and, if you carry on reading, I'll show you how to make it happen.

Secondly, it means taking responsibility for the stories you're telling yourself, it means stopping being the victim and blaming others. Making this change will enable you to move forward with your life and to find joy. If you carry on reading, you'll learn how to do this too.

And thirdly, it means being honest with others about who you are and the truth of your life. This doesn't mean telling your story to the world, perhaps it's opening up a bit to friends or family in a gentle and safe way.

I spoke to **Beverly Glick,** a Story Archaeologist about what she understands about owning your story.

> Own can mean many different things. In this context for me it means 'to have mastery', 'to be in command' and 'to have authority over'. If you have authority over your story, it means quite simply you are the author, and if you are the author of your story, you can rewrite it. That's why owning your story is important.
>
> Owning could also mean looking at owning our story as owning all parts of self and owning everything that we are. And speaking up about all the pieces of ourselves that make us unique.

I can totally empathise why it's so hard to own a difficult story, and I know that sometimes the fear of feeling the pain can be worse than the pain itself. Certainly that was my experience when I confronted my own story around grief. For me, holding it back was far more painful than feeling it. I very much understand the fear that people have around facing their own story let alone sharing it with anyone.

Maybe you've taken a big deep breath and recoiled, or perhaps you can see this as a gentle invitation to reconnect with yourself and with life. Because we both know that you're not *really* living now, are you?

I too held my story inside because initially it felt safe, but having this *big* secret damaged so many important friendships. Owning my story and telling it openly, has enabled me to integrate it into my life, and without this big secret many of my friendships are now deeper.

Writing Your Own Brave Ending

This is my wish for you and why I've written this book. At the end of our time together, if you work through the questions you'll be able to say *'yes I am childless. It has been incredibly hard and I felt completely alone. Even though I won't have the life I used to dream of, I know how I can have a fulfilling life'*. To do this you'll need to let go of some stories, and walk through Act Two. Then, you will be another step closer to the fulfilling life that is yours for the taking.

Your experience so far tells you that you can't control the story of your life but you *can* control your character in it. In fact who you are, your character, and who you will become are the *only* things you can control. I ask you to place your trust not just in me, but in the other women who've bravely taken control of their stories and shared them so that you can learn from what they did and take control of your story and your life.

Journaling Questions

- What are the key things you've learned from this chapter? Which areas would be helpful for you to explore further? Explore these as you write in your journal.

If you're not sure whether you want to answer the call, here are a few questions to assist you.

- What would my life be without this story?

- Who could I be without it?

- Who was I before I was childless?

- Where in my life am I using the language of impossibility?

- Are there other things I'm telling myself that I can't do?

- How could I let go of these stories?

- Which stories could I change to a probable or possible?

- And: What gifts could come to me if I do the thing I think I cannot do?

Will you join me and write your brave new ending?

Chapter Two

Setting The Scene How We Arrived In This Place Called Childless

What in your life is calling you,
When all the noise is silenced,
The meetings adjourned...
The lists laid aside,
And the Wild Iris blooms
By itself
In the dark forest...
What still pulls on your soul?

Rumi

Read the above quote again, and pause for a moment. How closely does it describe how you feel about your life?

I've been in that forest each time I've grieved. At first it felt dark and lonely and I imagined that I'd never be able to find my way out. Then after a while, I listened and could hear a quiet voice calling me forward. It was others who had been here before me, and laid down a path to help me find my way.

In the following pages you will read, in their own words how our storytellers came to be in the forest, and the many routes they travelled to this place we call childless. For now, I've ended each story in the forest, and the one thing to know before you start is that they have all worked their way out. All these women were broken and grieving for the life they couldn't have. They took their courage in both hands and pulled themselves back together in different ways.

I encourage you to read them all, even if they appear to be completely different to yours. Initially some will resonate with you more than others and before you stop reading, consider this. What if each one is your story, narrated by someone else?

One word of caution, reading them may cause some tears. I suggest you find yourself some privacy, get yourself a beverage of choice, a box of tissues, and then settle down.

Other than stating their name and where they live, I haven't introduced the storytellers as I believe their story tells you everything you need to know. The majority have chosen to use their real name and you might recognise some of them because you've read their book or blog. Others will be new to you; most of these shared their story for the first time on my blog. You'll read more of each story as you work through the book and those who can provide support are listed in the Resources Section. They are listed below in alphabetical order.

August — England

Over the course of two years we tried and failed to become pregnant. As each month passed, everything became increasingly stressful, punctuated by the stab of pain each period brought – the disappointment, the resentment at everyone else's apparent ease at getting pregnant, and feeling crushed by the guilt and weight of expectation from want-to-be grandparents. I was becoming very low (how much so I had no idea until much, much later). The physical and emotional relationship between my husband and myself was starting to suffer.

There followed three years of failed IVF attempts. Neither of us had appreciated or were prepared for how hard IVF would be. And it turned out to be the biggest hurt either of us had ever felt. I felt disappointed and cheated by life. I felt tricked on to a life path that was now never going to reach fulfilment. And, if that part of the dream wasn't going to happen, did I still want the rest of it?

Rapidly, and with everyone sadly noticing but me, I was falling to pieces. I applied for voluntary redundancy, as I knew I couldn't take any more – of work, of IVF, of my life, I wasn't sure – I just knew I wanted out.

Removing myself from the only things that had been anchoring me resulted in me going in to free fall. I felt like a big, useless void of a being, with no useful purpose in the world, and no recollection of whose life I now found myself in, or how I had ended up in it.

My relationship with my husband took a bit of a nosedive. I felt resentful to now be trapped in a marriage that would no longer play out as we had planned. I spent less and less time at home. I couldn't recognise any of the things I was surrounded by, and certainly didn't care about them anymore.

During this period I felt that I was about to 'break'. I felt very ill, but psychologically not physically. I eventually went to see my doctor who diagnosed me with depression and gave me medication. Things at home were being decimated by my state of mind and the dreadful atmosphere it was creating.

Both my husband and I were very, very unhappy, and for lack of knowing what else to do to stop the pain we were both feeling, I moved out into an apartment. We never discussed it being a permanent thing – just a thing that needed to happen right then, as we could not continue to go on as we were. I spent a lot of time away from my husband and friends, feeling very vulnerable and very lost. Things for my husband were no better, but I didn't have the capacity to help either of us at that point.

In the end, and finding myself at a loss as to what to now do with my life, I got the opportunity to go travelling (something I had always longed to do.) I spent two extended periods over the course of the next two years, seeing a bit of the world. This helped me gain some clarity about what had gone before, and made me realise how much I missed my husband. When I returned from my second trip, I moved back in and we agreed we would give things another go. The depression, and the reasons for it, had turned me into a person neither of us recognised for a while – but the old me seemed to be re-emerging to some degree.

Shortly after getting home I stopped taking my antidepressants and started to try and re-engage with my marriage and my life. I couldn't, however, re-engage with work. I still haven't fully.

Cali Bird — England

I was the archetypal Bridget Jones career girl living in London. I did have an opportunity to get married in my early twenties and, for various reasons, said no to it. As a teenager and young adult I wasn't bothered about having children. I loved my London life and was busy building my career, travelling, and having a lot of fun. From my mid-twenties I started pining for that special someone to settle down with though in truth, I don't think I was ready to settle down. I just *thought* I was.

When I was 29 a maternal urge kicked in. My body suddenly felt as though it wanted to have children but I was rocking up to 30 with no husband in sight.

During my thirties a lot of my friends got married and some started to have children. I found this very hard as my body seemed to be screaming to have a baby but there was no one to have it with. I didn't seem to have the skill to pick a nice man and form a relationship. I was single most of the time and any relationship that came along only lasted three or four months. I fell in love with one of my co-workers and, at the time, would have loved to have settled down and had his babies but he just wanted to keep things on a 'friends' basis and not be more involved.

It took me years to get over him. On one hand, in my thirties, I was having a blast. I lived in Central London, I earned good money and I had a very full life. On the other hand, there was always sadness and frustration that I was single and that my biological clock was ticking ever louder.

When I was 38 I considered having a child by what I called 21st century methods, such as with donor sperm. I gave myself a year to think about this, knowing that I shouldn't rush into it. During the course of that year I realised that what I wanted more was a partner and the partnership that it would bring. I didn't want to have a baby outside of this.

Approaching 40 I met the man who is now my husband. We were at school together though we weren't romantically involved back then. We knew very early on in our relationship that we had the potential for marriage, but he also told me that he didn't want to have children. His parents had been in their 40s when he was born and he didn't want to be an older parent.

Having spent all my thirties miserably yearning for what I didn't have, I didn't want to continue this. So I had a choice, I could be happy with what I had or continue to pine despondently for a child. I chose the former and have never looked back.

Christine Bishop — England, now New Zealand

I was one of those little girls who always wanted to be a mother. There was never any doubt in my mind that I wanted to get married and have children; only doubt that I might never meet a man who wanted to marry me! Fortunately that changed when I met my future husband at the relatively early age of 21 and we were married two years later at age 23. So there was no rush, we wanted to enjoy being just the two of us for a while before settling down to the responsibility of parenthood.

Then as 30 approached I got the opportunity of redundancy from my job in London, which was perfect as I wanted to stay at home with my children rather than go back to work. We had our perfect house and could afford to survive on one salary so the stage was all set.

Then nothing happened and after about a year we went to see our GP who said that they would refer us to a specialist but that it would take a while for the appointment to come through and in the meantime just relax and by then I would probably be pregnant anyway!

Sure enough, by the time the appointment came through I had just had a positive pregnancy test so no problem – until I miscarried a couple of weeks later. This was of course devastating but I was still young and if I could get pregnant once then I could again, and sure enough five months later another positive pregnancy test. However this also ended in miscarriage.

We went to see a specialist and I told her that I was an only child and that my mother had had several miscarriages before having me and asked if there could be any connection. Her response was that miscarriages weren't looked into until you'd had three and then they would investigate further. We then had several months on Clomid (a fertility drug) but there were no further pregnancies. We were then told we should do IVF.

Eventually we had a chromosome blood test and I was found to have a chromosome translocation (abnormality), which was completely devastating and our only realistic option was to try IVF with donor eggs. We decided to try and after being on a waiting list for a year we got our turn. Two eggs were fertilised and implanted but no pregnancy resulted.

We then heard about a revolutionary new treatment, which would mean doing IVF with my own eggs but removing a cell from any that fertilised to test for the chromosome translocation. We decided to give it a try so that we could then say that we had tried everything we could. The treatment resulted in seven eggs, five of which fertilised and were tested but each one was found to carry the translocation. So that was it, the end of the road.

We contemplated trying again, but aside from the financial and emotional cost, I was 42 and on discussing it we felt that while we desperately wanted it to be successful, we were also scared and worried about how we would cope with a baby at our age. So we decided to call it a day. We discussed adoption but decided that it was not for us for a variety of reasons.

> This was the lowest point of my life because, as well as the grief of coming to terms with not having a family, my mother had also passed away two years previously.

Emily Jacob — England

> When I was newly married at 24 I was diagnosed with polycystic ovaries syndrome (PCOS), which I'd most likely had since my periods started when I was ten. The consultant advised my husband and I to start trying for a family straight away because it might not happen. Except, because there was a possibility that it could – and we were both young and at the start of our careers (at that time, enjoying our relationship unencumbered) – I stayed on the pill for most of my twenties.
>
> Approaching 30, we started thinking about children. For a while we were trying very hard for children. Of course, that does actually involve having lots of sex, so we probably weren't trying that hard after all. I remember though being so green with envy at the seemingly unending parade of women at work with their pregnant bellies. There was even a (short) period where I understood how a woman might get to the point where she could steal another's baby for her own.
>
> When we divorced I was 34 and as part of moving on from that, I made a conscious decision that I was going to choose not to want children. My reasoning was that I was 34, I had been married for ten years, so I needed to meet someone, fall in love, get married, and be with them for more than ten years before I was going to trust 'forever' which I needed to decide to have children with them. Hence, the timing would be impossible, therefore better not to want.

A year later I was raped and my life took a very different turn. My focus was on survival and trying to recover my mental health.

The irony is that after my entire lifetime of periods, 24 years, of very irregular periods, sometimes only 3 or so a year, as soon as I divorced my husband, my periods became really regular, settling in to about 31-35 days. It would seem my body knew what I didn't; he wasn't the man for me.

About 3-4 years after the rape, I was still suffering from depression and from regular panic attacks. I hadn't quite had my major breakdown yet, but I decided moving into 2012 that I was going to change the script inside my head, stop myself and my problems being my only focus, and have a baby. I was going to be 39 that year and I wanted a baby before I was 40 and it was 'too late.' The fact that I wasn't even seeing a man at the time wasn't going to stop me. I bought myself a 3 for 2 deal on IUI and sperm donation.

They didn't take. Probably not a surprise, since I did have my breakdown that same year, and ended up back in counselling for the PTSD, eventually being under the care of a psychiatrist for 18 months.

Eventually, when I realised I had passed the age cut-off for my local council to fund IVF, I chose not to go into debt and fund it myself. And that left me with a feeling that maybe I didn't want my child enough, a guilt that I still feel a pull on today.

Enza Gandolfo — Australia

I was in my early 30s, and had been married for a couple of years, when we decided to start trying to have a child. Up until that point I had not been sure whether I wanted children or not and certainly in my 20s I was sure I would *not* have children. But finding myself in a relationship with a man I loved (and still love) and trusted who I knew would be a good father, I decided now was the time. I had my first miscarriage before I even knew I was pregnant. In the five years that followed I had a number of miscarriages and continual struggles with getting pregnant. Each time was more upsetting and difficult to deal with, each time was followed by more tests and testing until finally they diagnosed antiphospholipid antibody syndrome (an autoimmune condition). However, even with the diagnoses and the heparin injections, the next pregnancy ended in miscarriage.

By that stage I was feeling worn out and overwhelmed by grief. Some days I could not even bear to go out. It seemed like there were pregnant women everywhere. Every other woman seemed to be able to get pregnant but me. I couldn't think about anything else. I found it difficult to do anything else.

There was some pressure from doctors to go on IVF, 'if you really want to have children', one doctor said, implying I was not trying hard enough. Some of my family thought I should keep trying. But I knew that it was time to stop. We think we can control everything but we can't and sometimes in life it's about coming to terms with that.

I decided to stop trying and to write about my experience so that it might make a difference to other women. Later, I discovered that I was already premenopausal by that stage (but the doctors had not picked it up) and so it is likely that IVF would have resulted in more disappointment.

Helen Rebello — England

I met my gorgeous soulmate when I was 30, having spent 3 years living alone, getting to know myself and working out what I wanted in life – which certainly wasn't children! I remember having a conversation with him about it not long after we met, and worrying about the fact that even though I knew in my gut that he was 'the one', our views on having children were very different – and I didn't know how we would transcend that.

Life likes to play games of course, so this all changed completely when I was utterly taken over by the unstoppable force of the 'baby-blues' a couple of years later. By this time we were married and I was working as a Sonographer, scanning babies all day and working with those going through fertility problems. I became pregnant after what seemed like forever and six weeks of complete terror/excitement followed before I miscarried.

This was really hard, but despite the baby time-clock ticking away and driving me, at the back of my mind I still wasn't sure whether I had been committed enough to having a baby – so I blamed myself for not wanting the baby enough and that's why it didn't work out. A year later, the same thing happened again. It was easier this time, but still gut-wrenching.

By this time, most of my friends were now mothers and I was the last one without a child. At the time I wasn't sure which hurt more – the fact that I didn't have a baby, or the fact that I was the only one amongst them that remembered how it felt to be on that side of the fence as they all started to forget.

To cut a very long story short, I then found out that I had a 20cm fibroid indenting my endometrium (womb lining), and had a Myomectomy to remove the fibroid in the hope that I could then sustain a pregnancy. A long time later with no pregnancy in sight I took the difficult decision to have IVF after a friend asked me 'would you regret it in ten years' time if you didn't' (yes, I probably would have!). The day before the consultation, I found out I was pregnant – so the IVF was obviously delayed – until I found out I had an ectopic pregnancy and we started the whole journey again…

I eventually went back for IVF and found out at egg collection that I had a huge polyp at the entrance to my cervix – so the IVF was cancelled and the eggs were frozen whilst I had yet more surgery. By this time I was convinced that 'someone' was trying to tell me something – as things kept happening to stall the IVF (by this time I'd had about seven Gynae Ops)– but we had eggs frozen, so eventually we went back to complete the journey we had started – which as you're reading this, you know ended there.

All this took several years, and for most of the journey I had no one to talk to that understood, other than my husband. Most of my friends were too embarrassed to ask, or I did a good job of pretending I was okay, being too 'constrained' to volunteer the info. I felt embarrassed to talk about it, and was very hard on myself and my inability to 'get over it'. I didn't want to burden other people with my 'stuff'…

Eventually I left my job as a Sonographer and luckily for me, being forced to re-examine my job and my life was my salvation, as it started a path of self-discovery and learning a whole new way of being. Several years and lots of training and evolving later, I have 'birthed' a very different life and a much more nourishing way of helping others.

Helen G— England

Marrying at the age of 32 did feel quite late compared to my peers, but I had no idea that I was coming to the end of my most fertile stage in life – we both still felt so young. After trying to conceive for a year or so we decided we would see our GP. This led to tests, low level treatments, IUI and eventually to four cycles of IVF, all of which left us completely exhausted physically and emotionally. Although we briefly considered adoption, we just couldn't cope with more waiting and hoping.

During this intense time of treatment, I remember thinking many times that couples who conceived naturally had no idea how lucky they were. After turning away from any further treatment, we decided to continue trying to conceive without all the pressure and stress of medical intervention. We also saw a nutritionist and after about a year or so I did actually conceive but sadly it was over before it had begun. The final straw for me was my colleague announcing she was pregnant, just as I was being told I wasn't and I knew then that we had to stop because I couldn't cope any more with the build-up of hope, the waiting, then the crushing disappointment.

I probably had mild depression after all of this and did have some counselling but most of the time I felt that I shouldn't be there, that I was just making a fuss and that I should pull myself together. At no time did any professional tell me that I was grieving and that was normal and okay. It wasn't until a friend said to me that not having children was like a bereavement then suddenly I felt I had been given the right to grieve and that I wasn't just being overly emotional. Most of the time though I was grieving alone.

My husband had an absorbing job to lose himself in but I felt that I didn't fit in anywhere. I felt outside of the Mum's club, unattractive, a failure as a woman and a failure with regard to my career (I had given up teaching, not able to give it the energy that it required). There was no Plan B and I just coasted along for ten or more years, putting on a brave face. With friends who had children, I'd always told them not to be worried about telling me they were pregnant or talking about their children because I didn't want to be cut off from them and excluded. I was also genuinely happy for them, but I realise now that I was very lonely and isolated. Although we knew other couples who had had IUI or IVF, all of them had been successful. There was no one in our situation.

Jessica Hepburn — England

I always wanted a career but I also always wanted children. I never contemplated that the two things could be mutually exclusive and did what many of my generation did – went to university, then spent my twenties pursuing my career and finding the right partner. By my early thirties I was running one of London's largest theatres and had met the man I wanted to have a family with. We began trying when I had just turned 34. I thought it was the perfect age to have your first baby but it was the beginning of what became a desperate decade long struggle to conceive, which involved eleven rounds of IVF.

I realise that this is the extreme end of the treatment spectrum but we were diagnosed with 'Unexplained Infertility', which meant that technically everything looked like it was working properly. Sadder still, we seemed to be able to make perfect embryos yet I couldn't get pregnant. We went through several biomedical pregnancies; an ectopic pregnancy only discovered at three months; and a miscarriage after we'd seen a foetal heartbeat. Doctors told us these were all very good signs that if we kept trying it would eventually work – and I'm not very good at giving up – so we did. But sadly nature had other plans!

Jill Duffin — England

I met my future husband when I was 22 and we moved in together 2 years later and enjoyed our childfree existence. I qualified as a librarian and was building a career in the commercial sector. When I was 28, we decided we wanted a bigger house and we moved to the Surrey/Sussex borders. I changed jobs soon after moving. While the job seemed exciting with foreign travel, the long hours and commute began to affect me. We decided that I would join my husband in his new business that he was ready to expand. We worked long hours together and were under considerable financial strain. Friends were settling down and starting to have children, and when I was 33 we decided to get married and start trying for a family.

The first year nothing happened. Eventually we went to the doctor and started the round of infertility tests. It was rather a shock 18 months on to be diagnosed with stage 4 endometriosis, the severest kind. I was now aware that the biological clock was ticking.

The next seven years we really felt like we were on a merry-go-round of me taking drugs or going through surgery to keep the endometriosis at bay followed by another round of IVF. I felt reasonably positive about our success rates and kept a picture of twins by my bedside. We looked at the statistics for IVF and decided to have five attempts as figures showed a 20% chance of success.

Our fifth try was not a success; I stopped the treatment as I produced one poor quality egg. We made the decision to give it our best shot and have a final sixth attempt; by this stage I was 41. On our final IVF, 3 embryos were put back; I had a borderline pregnancy test, which probably meant that the embryo died.

Emotionally and financially we knew it was time to stop. We did not feel donor eggs were right for us and we looked in to adoption, but I felt too vulnerable to proceed. It was a low time for us both and I realised working from home was not doing my emotional well-being any good. Fortunately my husband had the chance of going into partnership with another company and we made the decision to sell our dream house and move back to London.

Although not relishing returning to work, I was falling into depression being at home on my own. I knew that I excelled at my first career and made the decision to return. I took the first job I was offered. It was in the suburbs and all the women I worked with had children, so it was not the best return for me. Fortunately a year later I was offered a job at a not for profit organisation back in London. It was great to be working with a young team and I had a good social life – making up for the last seven years.

I was often down in the beginning, but I knew it helped to be busy and doing something that I loved. Four years later I was offered my dream job, combining information and advice at a membership organisation. Although the role eventually changed with a restructure I was there for seven happy years, by which time I knew I was ready for new challenges.

Jody Day — England, now Ireland

I got married young (although I thought I was very grown-up at the time) at twenty-six. My husband, seven years older than me, was a charming, glamorous fashion designer and we were madly in love. I wasn't completely sure I wanted children when we married and I told my husband-to-be so; having had a pretty disrupted childhood myself, 'family life' wasn't my idea of fun.

But gradually I got used to the idea, and because it was no longer an abstract notion of 'children', but a child who would be the product of our love and made up of our combined DNA, when I was twenty-nine we started trying for a family. I didn't get pregnant straight away but I wasn't too concerned; I'd had an abortion at twenty, which, although it was pretty traumatic emotionally (I was terrified of having a baby as one of the messages I'd internalized from family, school and wider society was that 'children ruin your life') at least it reassured me that 'everything worked'. I was more confused than anything else at my inability to get pregnant because it didn't fit in with my plans – and I was a ferocious planner in those days! I cringe to admit it now but I had a chart listing month-by-month my plans for the next five years of my life, including which months I planned to conceive so that our children's births would fit around our schedule. I still have that month-by-month planner in a box somewhere. I keep it to remind me how much I've changed, and how I no longer expect life to go according to my plans.

At the age of 33, and 4 years into trying for a baby, I had a laparoscopy under general anaesthetic – a procedure in which a camera is inserted through your navel to take a look around the reproductive system. 'Ready to move into!' said my avuncular gynaecologist as I came round from the anaesthetic. 'Excellent property! Nothing to worry about!' All our tests on hormones, sperm counts, etc., came back fine too. Looking back on it now, I can't quite believe that after trying to conceive for four years, IVF wasn't even mentioned to us by the doctors, nor was I given any advice about the fact that I only had two years before I turned 35 and my fertility statistically fell off a cliff. They reassured us that everything was fine, that there was no damage from the abortion, and I was happy to take that at face value.

Over the coming years, we kept on trying (the only advice we ever got from doctors) and I saw every nutritionist, herbalist, acupuncturist, shaman, healer, homoeopath, naturopath, and quack in London. I tried every diet, made all the lifestyle changes and became an expert on my ovulation dates, peeing on every colour and type of stick I could buy. Yet, each month, regular as clockwork, my period would come and I'd be in tears once more.

The doctors called it 'unexplained infertility' and left it at that, never mentioning that we may have been eligible for one or two rounds of IVF treatment paid for by our local health authority. We did briefly consider IVF, but couldn't afford it privately and I was very wary of it too – I really didn't like the idea of the hormone treatments and I was convinced I'd conceive naturally anyway; I mean absolutely, unshakably *convinced*.

All these years later and with the benefit of hindsight, I can see that perhaps my earlier ambivalence over having a family may have found a new home – in my anti-IVF stance. By the time I was ready to consider IVF, at 37, our marriage was on its last legs. By the time I was 38, our marriage was over, suffocated by the combined weight of his alcoholism and workaholism and my co-dependency and infertility.

Astonishingly, I still thought there was plenty of time left for me to have a family! I reasoned that because I was young-looking for my age, that my periods were regular as clockwork and that I felt myself ovulating every month, it must have been my husband. On a conscious level, I gave it no more thought and set my mind to getting divorced as quickly as possible and moving on. Around 40, I started dating again, and just before my 41st birthday, my ex-husband got a casual girlfriend accidentally pregnant. She either didn't keep the baby or had a very early miscarriage – I can't remember now, the details are hazy with distress. But I do recall how the knowledge of this absolutely devastated me because I could no longer hold on to the fantasy that somehow things were going to work out 'naturally' for me.

In the next few years I had a couple of serious relationships, but sadly neither of them were stable enough to consider doing IVF. And so, when my most serious post-divorce relationship ended, I was forty-four years old. Well, forty-four and a half actually!

I remember a gloomy, rainy February afternoon in the grotty studio flat I'd moved into after a stormy and distressing break-up. I was standing watching the rain on the window when the traffic in the street seemed to become completely muted. In that moment, I became acutely aware of myself, standing there, looking out of the window. And then it came to me:

It's over. I'm never going to have a baby.

I realised with absolute clarity and complete certainty that even if I were to meet a new partner immediately, we'd need to be together for at least a year before we could even think about doing IVF. It was too late for that. I was too old. It was over. I was never going to have a baby.

Johanna Walker — USA

When I was ten, I started orchestrating my wedding. We bought a house, had children and lived happily ever after. The end.

Cathy Glen my friend declared she wasn't going to get married and have children. I looked at her in dismay, we're girls; don't all girls have children? In my family and culture the Promised Land was marriage and children.

I spent my 20s and 30s trying to unravel that story. I did many different things and I did not get married and I did not have children. Yet. As I approached 40 I started to think – wow, maybe I'm not going to have kids. This was a novel though as I always figured I would eventually have them.

I had a pretty good look at parenting and wasn't sure if that was what I wanted in my life. I considered the possibility of not having children and it was okay. I recognised there would be some grieving to do, but it was okay.

But here's the thing. I was always told, '*when* you...' not '*if* you...' and those words stick to the bones. It was difficult to separate the programming and expectations that got laid on me so heavily from my authentic desires. By the time I'd teased these apart and I could hear the still small voice that said 'maybe I want to have a child'. It was too late.

Although I knew I'd have to grieve, I had no idea of the magnitude of it or what that was going to mean emotionally. The grieving knocked me over. It almost killed me. I was not going to the Promised Land and I couldn't tell that there was anywhere else worth going to.

Karen Malone Wright — USA

As an only child, I dreamed of one day having a huge family. *Cheaper by the Dozen* was one of my favourite movies; *The Waltons* and *Eight Is Enough* were among my favourite TV shows. I learned that I was the result of an unplanned pregnancy when my mother was in college. My father was not the man she'd hoped to marry. She married my dad, and she loved me, but my existence meant she'd never have the life she'd dreamed of.

Soon after college, I became pregnant by the man I thought was the love of my life. When I told him, he asked me whose baby it was. Our relationship didn't last long after that, and I had an abortion. In the late '80s, I married a man 12 years older than me with a grown daughter from a previous marriage. She had a two-year-old, making me a stepmother and step-grandmother before I ever gave birth myself. I divorced him after four years, with no regrets.

I remarried and hoped to have a child, but when my period arrived each month, I realized that a part of me was relieved. The older you get, the more you understand the sacrifices that motherhood requires. At 44, I was diagnosed with Type 2 diabetes and my gynaecologist told me that my chances of a successful pregnancy were very low. The news sent me into a horrible depression that lasted for years. What had been ambivalence about having a child turned in to an overwhelming sadness that had me leaving baby showers early and crying at the sight of a pregnant woman's belly. I wondered if I'd ever overcome the grief.

The Internet was young then: 'social' meant 'chat rooms', and the only ones I could find for childless women focused on infertility, IVF, and miscarriage, and I didn't fit in any of them. At my workplace and in my community, women without kids were hard to find.

Linda Rooney — New Zealand

The short version is that my husband and I waited till I was in my mid-30s to start to try to have children. I had a busy international career, but it wasn't just about the career. I thought it was important to have children when I was ready, and not before. I wanted to be a mother that was fully present for her children, not resentful of her stolen youth. I also wanted to feel the maternal urge, and it ambled up to me in my mid-30s.

By the time I first conceived, I was in its full grip. Whether it was simply biology (hormones and that ticking clock), my own natural wishes at the right time, or peer pressure, I don't know and will never know. But I had a deep and genuine desire to be a mother.

Of course, as is obvious now, it's not that easy. The short version of my story is that two ectopic pregnancies and two failed IVFs later, I knew I would never have children. I got the news on my 41st birthday. I've had better birthdays.

Lisa Manterfield — USA

I was in my mid-30s when I met my husband (aka Mr. Fab.) He has two grown children, so we talked very early in our relationship and agreed that having children together was an experience we wanted to share. He underwent vasectomy reversal surgery (they don't call him Mr. Fab for nothing) so we knew we might have some problems getting pregnant and we talked about how far we were willing to go to make it work. We both favour natural and holistic medicine, where possible, and neither of us was comfortable with the amount of drugs needed for IVF.

As it turned out, Mr. Fab's fertility wasn't the problem at all, and IVF wasn't something that would have even worked for us. We spent several years dotting around between acupuncturists and fertility clinics before I was finally diagnosed with Primary Ovarian Insufficiency (POI) and told my best chance of pregnancy was via egg donation.

For many reasons, that wasn't something we wanted to do, and we would have opted for adoption instead. However, by the time we reached that stage we were already emotionally exhausted and we needed a break. We went through several cycles of taking a break and then getting back on the train again, because I'd read about a new potential treatment or picked up a new book by a doctor who'd performed miracles with Chinese medicine, but ultimately we took a month off to regroup, which became six months, then a year, and so on. We fizzled out rather than hit a wall.

Liz Ascham — England

As far back as I can remember, I have always wanted to be a mum and always told people that was what I wanted to be when I grew up. I was devastated when, at 24, I was told, following years of uncertainty and tests, that I had gone through menopause. It completely changed my life and for many years I struggled with relationships and coming to terms with my diagnosis. As a children's nurse, I spent a lot of time with children and, in retrospect, this helped me but equally reminded me of what I couldn't have.

Over the years, I have become an Auntie, a Godmother and a significant adult to many children, for which I'm very grateful. It has been a hard journey, and one which I could not have made without the love and support of my wonderful parents, family, and friends who have all helped and listened to me over the years.

When Steve and I decided to get married, during our year travelling through Central and South America, we also decided that we would try to have a baby through IVF and egg donation. On our return to England, another journey started, which seemed to take over. Sadly, it wasn't successful.

However, a few years on, I'm delighted to say that Steve and I are very happy and enjoy ourselves, despite being childless, and we have discovered many things to fill our lives.

Louise — England

Let's start at my wedding day when I was surrounded by love of my tall, dark, and handsome husband, Andrew, his family, my family and all our friends. It was perfect. I was 27, Andrew at 26 was my toy boy by six months and we thought waiting two years before we starting trying for our family of four would give us time to buy a house, decorate it and feel ready to settle down properly.

As an eldest child, I am law abiding and sensible so I followed the good advice of waiting six months after coming off the pill before going for gold. Three years later, and many excuses to ourselves, there was still no medal in sight.

We took three months of work, went on a trip to Australia and New Zealand and came back ready to start again. Another 18 months after we returned and realising the excuses preventing us from going to the doctors, I finally found myself on the operating table for the first of many different treatments, explorations, or whatever else you want to call them. Another year later and we were in a lecture hall at St Thomas Hospital in London listening to the fertility team explain how IVF worked, what the pills and potions were, and what the success rates were. I simply felt overwhelmed. As we walked towards the hospital I had stopped, cried and said 'I can't go in'. I just did not want to be one of those people who could not have a baby in the way that nature intended.

Five rounds of IVF, a few more investigations and procedures along the way, and never a blue line in sight, in May 2002 a week after my 39th birthday we had to accept that the dream was over. I had a low ovarian reserve while Andrew had super sperm. So, it was all my fault in my eyes. How do you pick yourself up from such a low point? How do you start to build a new life? That was the big question. At one stage during our treatment, when I was very frustrated I shouted 'why don't you leave me for someone who can give you children?' Andrew swore he would never do that but in early August he told me he needed space and was going to move out for 'a couple of weeks, to give us space'. He left in October and didn't return for almost a year. We had drifted apart while on the IVF roller coaster and as time went on, he went out more as by nature he cannot sit still and needs people, music, noise. On the other hand I stayed in more being someone who has to work through things on her own before being ready to face the world again.

While we were apart we tried to patch things but and went to see Relate. It took more than three months to secure the first appointment and I often felt the counsellor took Andrew's side rather than being impartial. On one occasion she told me she thought I was looking for compensation for not having children. Through my tears I managed to spit out the words 'I can never be compensated for this'. Although I am now stronger and have a completely new life, it is still not compensation for the life I wanted. I have accepted that I cannot control everything or have everything I want. I simply have to enjoy what I do have, count my blessings, and be grateful for all the ways in which I can now share in the lives of my nieces, nephews and Godchildren.

Andrew came home and we spent two more years together. It was really nothing more than sharing a house. Despite my attempts to fool myself and others, it was no great surprise when he left for good in January 2006. It was almost another three years before I discovered he had left me for a younger model.

Very, very slowly and surrounded by friends and family I slowly picked myself. I spent weekends hiding away; leaving the curtains closed; refusing to answer the phone; eating if I wanted to; and generally letting life go by in a fog. At work, I told my boss and a couple of close friends what had happened otherwise I ploughed on as usual not telling anyone what had happened until a whole year later. I never lied when anyone asked me what we were doing at the weekend, I simply replied 'I am doing' whatever it was.

Just before Christmas 2008 Andrew told me that there was new partner and then went on to say, 'there's a child. It's seven months old'. His choice of words seemed incredibly cold. I amazed myself and congratulated him.

This revelation temporarily sent me back round the roller coaster but with each passing year or each new hurdle I face, the dips are shallower and I can rise again like a phoenix from the ashes much more quickly.

As for next steps on my journey, I hope that one day I will meet someone to share my life with. At first I could not imagine this. Now I'm almost ready to chance the heartbreak again.

Pamela Mahoney Tsigdinos — USA

I came of age in the early days of the second wave of the women's movement and grew up in the heady times when women, for the first time, could look ahead without fear of limits or dead ends. Like most women I took my fertility for granted in my 20s. That's what made learning in my early 30s, that getting pregnant might not be as easy as our Sex Ed teachers made it seem, more than a bit of a shock.

Prior to 'Dr Google' and all the online communities, I was left to my own devices to figure out what was wrong. My husband and I fell into the maddening 'unexplained infertility' category. We tried natural, organic, and herbal remedies as well as advanced science with multiple surgeries and treatments – all of which failed. By the numbers, it was more than 20 years since I first tried to get pregnant, 10 years since I walked away from fertility medicine, and eight years more to stop wondering if a miracle pregnancy would occur.

I was 43 when I first let go of my dreams of motherhood and began re-architecting my life and my expectations about who I would become and how my life might unfold.

Rosalind Bubb — England

I was thirty-two and we'd been married for four years, when we decided to try to have a family. I became pregnant after four months. At seven weeks there were signs that all might not be well. I phoned NHS Direct and the lady I spoke to suggested resting in bed. I spent a gruelling week there, wishing and hoping that it would all be okay. At the end of that week my GP sent me for a scan, which showed that the baby had died two weeks earlier. A natural miscarriage eventually followed. I felt as if my heart had broken.

My next pregnancy went to eight weeks until a scan revealed that it was ectopic. After a tortuous week of monitoring hormone levels, I was given a drug which caused the foetus to be reabsorbed, and I effectively had another miscarriage.

My third pregnancy seemed to be fine. My twelve week scan was delayed to fourteen weeks, and I had the biggest shock of my life, when they told us the baby had no heartbeat. The next day I had an operation to remove the baby's remains, but it didn't go well and I lost a great deal of blood from my womb, and I ended up staying in hospital. Two days after I came home, my husband flew to the other side of the world to deliver a training course, which was staggeringly hard to deal with. I felt as if my heart had been broken again, and this miscarriage took a lot longer to get over.

Two weeks before my scan, I had been taught to use EFT 'tapping' (Emotional Freedom Techniques) and I used this on myself throughout the whole experience, tapping for hours each day. This reduced the distress somewhat, and made me feel able to face each step. I honestly don't know how I would have got through it all, without it.

Once I'd begun to recover, I started to train intensively in EFT 'tapping'. I added it to my existing practice as a hypnotherapist and NLP practitioner, and I gradually found myself doing most of my client work with it. As I became more and more highly trained, I used 'tapping' systematically to clear the emotional pain, distress, and trauma from my many, many miscarriage memories.

After about six miscarriages, I discovered another very powerful therapeutic self-help tool, called TAT (Tapas Acupressure Technique), which facilitated the grieving process. On at least twenty occasions, I sat on my bed and did TAT and sobbed for twenty minutes. The feelings were pure grief; it didn't feel frightening or unpleasant. It felt absolutely the right thing to do. And all of the distressing miscarriage memories became more and more soft and gentle, on every occasion.

After unsuccessfully going through everything that the Recurrent Miscarriage Clinic in London had to offer, my eleventh pregnancy was through IVF. The private Harley Street clinic concluded that my immune system was attacking my embryos: they weren't the problem; it was 'the hostile environment.' The IVF involved three transfusions of very expensive, strong, immune suppressing drugs and I became pregnant… and then I miscarried again, in the summer shortly before my thirty-ninth birthday.

This miscarriage was also very difficult to get over and broke my heart. I had put everything I knew how, into trying to achieve a successful pregnancy. I had worked with my EFT teacher throughout it all, visualising every day, and trying to support my immune system to behave as we wanted it to. I had 'tapped' for two to three hours every day, for about two months. When it was time to put the embryos back into my womb, the doctor said he had never seen anyone as calm as me, and he asked me to write down how I'd done it, so that he could train in 'tapping' too, to help other patients.

So after this IVF miscarriage, my husband and I officially decided that we wouldn't make any decisions until the following spring. (We couldn't afford another round of IVF, and I also really couldn't contemplate trying that hard again.) But in fact I found this state of indecision and limbo to be unbearable, and in the autumn I felt as if I had a little mid-life crisis (although I don't think anyone else noticed!)

Over the course of three months I rapidly began actively to seek out women friends and acquaintances of mine who were childless, and I had positive conversations with them about how that was all right for them, and how it could be for me too. Although it wasn't a joint decision at that point, in my mind I began to embrace the possibility of being childless. And eventually, the following spring, my husband and I formally decided to stop trying for a family any more.

My fortieth birthday, that summer, was a very joyful affair. I was determined to put my attempts to have a baby in the past, and to embrace the next decade as one that did not involve this.

I didn't want the rest of my (theoretical) child-bearing years to be spent in this way. I was really pleased to be forty, and was pleased to say that 'enough is enough.' I had really tried. And now it was time to focus on the rest of my life.

Tracey Cleantis — USA

I remember the moment I got off the phone with my reproductive endocrinologist's office and telling them that I would not be doing any more treatment. It was a dark moment, major dark…the kind of dark that if it was a movie there would be cellos playing and violins instructing you to cry your eyes out. Only I required no such soundtrack to cue me, I was a wreck. It was over, I would no longer be trying to conceive and I would never be a parent to a biological child.

Yes, I was making the choice to quit trying; however, I was making the choice because I was at the bottom emotionally, physically, and there was no more money to spend on treatment. I had undergone four full rounds of IVF, twenty-something rounds of IUI (over half of those with injectables). While that sounds like a lot, it ain't nothing compared to how much non-traditional treatment I endured in order to conceive (acupuncture, nutritionists, chi gong practitioners, Maori chieftains, astrologers, healers, etc., etc.) Making the decision that I could endure no more was a hard one, but a necessary one for my emotional, mental, physical, and psychological well-being.

Apart from shedding a few tears, what do you read in these stories?

For me, I notice that they are like maps, showing many routes to the place in the forest we call childless. Whilst they are very personal they are also universal, demonstrating that how we feel when we arrive is very similar.

As I wrote earlier, each of these women pulled themselves back together and found their way out of the forest. Per Rumi's wise words at the start of the chapter, they became quiet, listened, and heard what was quietly pulling on their soul. So take heart beautiful reader, and know in your bones that you can find your way out of the forest too. If you read on I will show you how.

Journaling Questions

- What did you learn from these stories?

- Which ones resonated with you and why?

- Which didn't resonate with you? Explore the reasons for this in your journal.

- What do the storytellers have in common?

Chapter Three

Who Are You? Finding Your Light

I wish I could show you when you are lonely or in darkness the astonishing light of your own being.

Hafiz of Shiraz

I love this quote very much and I chose it because it summarises the aim of this chapter.

In Act Two I'm going to challenge you, but don't worry, you won't be going in empty-handed. As the quote from Hafiz of Shiraz says, you have an astonishing light inside. It's just that recent events have dimmed it a bit. To go back to the caterpillar, it has everything inside it to become a butterfly. So do you. But you may have forgotten, so in the remainder of Act One I'll remind you of who you are and show you how to find the light inside so it can illuminate your way.

What's Your Starting Point?

I can assure you that not everything in your life is negative. There are some areas of your life that are better than others, and we'll start by noticing these and at the same time you will work out your starting point. We'll do this with the Wheel of Life. Using this tool, you will gain insight into the balance of your life and how satisfied you are with the different areas. By considering each aspect of your life to be like a spoke of a wheel, you will see that those areas where you have scored low are throwing your whole life off balance.

Draw a wheel on a piece of paper (or download an example form the resources available on my website). Divide it into eight segments. Each one will represent a different area of your life. The list below contains a selection. Either choose the eight that are most important to you or add different ones, and write them into the wheel.

Area of life (examples)

Career / work / job / business	Fun / social life / friends
Money / finances	Home
Health / well-being / fitness	Family
Personal Development	Hobbies /creativity

Significant others / intimate relationships

The centre of the wheel represents a score of zero, the outside is ten. Score your level of satisfaction with each area of your life on a scale of zero to ten.

Join the dots to create a new wheel.

How bumpy is the ride? Spend a few moments reflecting on your scores for each section, all of them. Keep it to hand as you work through the book. We'll come back to it later.

Who Are You? The Importance of Values

As I've already written, this process of coming to terms with childlessness has thrown you off balance and what we're doing here is finding you again. In this section, we're going to dig into the essence of you, that light inside that has stayed the same throughout your life. This is what will carry you forward.

As you work through the questions in Act Two you will be rocked about a bit, knowing the light at your core will give you a sense of solidity and steadiness and also the courage to grow further.

What I mean by this light is your core values.

What are values?

Big picture – *a value is what is important to you in any given context*. They're usually single words and they guide everything you do. What you value determines what life means to you; they're the way you interpret what's important to you and what makes you feel good.

Values determine your drive and behaviour and can both motivate you and demotivate you. They affect your choice of friends, hobbies, interests, and how you spend your time; and if something doesn't fit with your values, you won't do it.

You may only become aware of them when they've been violated, (for example I get really annoyed when I see people dropping litter on the street) or when you become really passionate about something. The guilt you may feel if you let someone down is because you didn't meet your values.

Core values are a way of being or believing that you hold most important in your life and are unspoken rules and regulations by which you live. They're the backbone of your life, your guide, your map and compass, sometimes described as your 'North Star.' They are the essence of you, the core of who you are. Some may change over time particularly with life circumstances, which is why it's helpful to examine them regularly.

You will normally have around six core values and they are usually single words or short phrases, among them can be: *courage, making a difference, faith, love, compassion, fairness, fun, generosity, hope, kindness, peace, respect, recognition, spirituality, understanding, and wisdom.*

Here are examples of core values from two storytellers.

Louise: In many ways, I am still the girl I was at 18. My underlying values are the same. I still believe in fairness, honesty, truth, giving my all, and being the best that I can be without trampling on others.

Pamela Mahoney Tsigdinos: The author Elizabeth Gilbert sat down and wrote her truths. They were very straightforward and simple. I thought I'd try very hard to define my truths in plain English. For instance, this one: I am on a life path that's not better or worse than most women. It's just different. As I started to write my truths it became very evident that they had carried me through my whole life. There were few significant shifts.

There are certain characteristics that define us. One of my defining characteristics is that I'm somewhat of an anthropologist, a student of what makes us human. I want to understand myself in the world in which I live. I realise I've been like this since I was quite young. I try to understand not only myself and the people around me but how we react differently to the experiences we go through.

Why are they important?

When you identify your core values and live in a way that's aligned with them, something magical happens: you and they come alive in unexpected ways. You feel content, in harmony and you have peace of mind, even in challenging times. They serve as your internal compass and when you're living authentically with them you'll be moving closer to the life you really want.

Values light your way.

Knowing your core values and operating in alignment with them will encourage you to move forward with your life. Also if you want to do something challenging, you'll be okay as long as the action you take is in alignment with them.

In *Rising Strong,* Brené Brown uses going into the arena to describe doing something challenging. She says, *'there are no guarantees in the arena. We will struggle. We will fall. There will be darkness. But if we are clear about the values that guide us in our efforts to show up and be seen, we will always be able to find the light. We will know what it means to live brave'.*

As you work through this book, there may indeed be darkness and you will be challenged. Knowing your values will light your way. It's almost as if you don't have a choice. They'll compel you forward in magical ways that may not always be comfortable but will *feel* right.

My Story: So That's Why I Hated My Job; And Now...

Some things that really annoy me in life are dishonesty and unfair or unequal treatment. I didn't like my previous job working for a charity, and it was only when I learned about values that I realised why that was. I was one of four working for the same manager and in my eyes he treated me differently from the others.

My dad became ill and was in hospital for many weeks, 200 miles from where I lived. I asked to cut my hours in order to care for him and they refused to discuss options, ultimately calling me dishonest about why I wanted the time off. I felt personally violated to my core and resigned.

When I learned about values in my NLP training I realised how much there was a mismatch between mine and those of the charity. Well maybe not the professed values of the charity, but certainly those they operated by.

Now I live and work in alignment with my values. I see how much they light my way, give me an inner strength and help me to be authentic. They guide me to be who I want to be, and when I tell my truth from this place and I get criticised or others take a different view, I am okay.

Writing this book is in alignment with my values of making a difference, courage, and growth. It has stretched me to grow probably more than anything else I've ever done (and at the time of writing, I haven't started on publication and marketing yet), and every day it takes courage to dig deep, to write and to ask for help when I realise I'm stuck.

I have no idea whether or not the book will be successful (whatever that means), and whatever happens I will be okay because writing it is aligned with my values.

Journaling Questions

Finding your values.

Before you do the exercise below to find yours, here are a few words of advice:

You're aiming for around six words or short phrases. What each word means will be individual to you, for example what courage means to me, will be different to you.

If your initial list is longer than six, that's okay. Write them on a sheet of paper and, taking your time, reduce them to six. You might decide that some you circled aren't important, or that maybe some meanings overlap. For example, my initial list included adventure, travel, and learning. I decided to include growth on my list as it encompasses all of those.

I suggest you do this exercise over a few days and gradually refine the list so that by the end you have six words which describe the essence of you. If you gave them to a close friend, she would say 'yes that's you.'

There are two options.

Option One

Look at the list of values below and answer the question; 'what's really important to me?' Circle the words that jump out at you.

Acceptance	Creativity	Health	Legacy
Accountability	Curiosity	Home	Recognition
Achievement	Dignity	Honesty	Reliability
Adaptability	Diversity	Humility	Respect
Adventure	Efficiency	Humour	Resourcefulness
Ambition	Equality	Independence	Responsibility
Authenticity	Excellence	Integrity	Security
Balance	Fairness	Intuition	Self-respect
Belonging	Faith	Joy	Simplicity
Career	Family	Kindness	Spirituality
Caring	Financial stability	Knowledge	Success
Challenge	Flexibility	Leadership	Tradition
Collaboration	Forgiveness	Love	Travel
Community	Freedom	Loyalty	Trust
Compassion	Friendship	Making a Difference	Understanding
Competence	Fun	Openness	Usefulness
Confidence	Generosity	Optimism	Vision
Connection	Giving back	Nature	Vulnerability
Contentment	Grace	Patience	Wealth
Contribution	Gratitude	Peace	Well-being
Courage	Growth	Perseverance	Wholeheartedness
	Happiness	Personal Fulfilment	Wisdom

Option Two

If this hasn't quite worked, you may find it easier to answer some or all of the questions below. The key is to *remember a specific time*. Then once you have it, *go back specifically* to that time and really experience it. Remember exactly what you were doing, who you were with, and what you were seeing, hearing and feeling. Then answer the question.

Remember a specific time:

1. **When you were really motivated.**

    As you go back and remember that time, what was it that caused you to feel really motivated?

2. **When you felt real joy.**

    What caused you to feel that joy?

3. **When you felt that you'd achieved something that you felt proud of.**

    What caused you to feel proud?

4. **When you felt really angry.**

    What caused you to feel angry (the chances are one of your values was being violated)?

5. **When you felt really strongly about something (this could be a strong positive emotion such as love, happiness; or negative such as hate, or jealousy).**

    What caused you to feel this way?

6. **When you felt really guilty about something you did or didn't do.**

    What caused you to feel guilty (the chances are one of your values was being violated)?

Get creative.

Once you have your list you may wish to get creative and draw them on to a large sheet of paper, or find pictures that represent each of them. And if the word *creative* sends you into a tailspin, I understand. You can write them out, instead.

Mine are on a board behind my desk so they are always at the edge of my consciousness. You may also wish to keep them close by as you dig deep in Act Two. And remember they're not set in stone; we'll come back and take another look in Act Three.

Chapter Four

The First Step: Change Your Mind

Everything can be taken from a man but one thing: the last of the human freedoms – to choose one's attitude in any given set of circumstances, to choose one's own way.

Viktor E. Frankl

The powerful quote above explains the essence of this chapter. Frankl was an Austrian neurologist, psychiatrist, and Holocaust survivor who wrote about his experiences in *Man's Search for Meaning.*

The bottom line is *you and only you* have the choice to decide what sort of life you have. You can decide whether to continue being unhappy and imprisoned by the stories you tell yourself or you can let them go, and do the work so you can tell a new and more positive one. *You* have the power to make this choice. Claim it.

I've already explained how important story is to the life you have and one of the key ways to change the story you are telling is by talking to yourself in a positive way.

What Story Are You Choosing?

Let's dig into some theory.

Research by Professor Martin Seligman, an American psychologist, educator, and author proposed that each of us has our own 'explanatory style', a way of explaining to ourselves why things, good or bad, happen to us. We develop this during childhood and it stays the same throughout our life unless we deliberately change it. It acts as a lens through which we view the world and there are three elements to it: personalization, pervasiveness, and permanence. Let's call the two extremes, optimistic and pessimistic.

Personalization. Those with an optimistic style blame setbacks on external factors and are generally more confident, whereas pessimists generally have low self-esteem, blame themselves and view everything as their fault, they will say things like 'I could have...' or 'I should have...'

Pervasiveness. When things go wrong for pessimists, they see it as affecting (or pervading) all areas of their life whereas optimists see it as specific. The opposite is true for success in that optimists allow good events to brighten every area of their lives rather than just the particular area in which the event occurred.

Permanence. Pessimists assume that when something goes wrong, it will always go wrong whereas optimists will simply tell themselves that it was a temporary setback and will go better next time. The reverse is true for positive events: optimists believe good things happen for reasons that are permanent, rather than temporary.

Do you recognise these in yourself?

The important thing to note is that these are thinking styles, not personality traits and therefore can be changed.

Here are two stories to illustrate the extremes.

Janet stopped trying to have children five years ago and describes herself as a victim. She feels stuck and powerless to do anything, and depends on others to feel good about herself and about her life. She is often heard blaming others or saying things like 'If only (I'd done .....) then (my life would be great).' She often uses phrases such as 'I should/could do ...' but never does what she says. She believes that she *is* a failure, and not being able to have children means she's failed in all areas of life. She often says that she'll always feel this way and will never be happy.

She feels like she's a passenger in a car, not in control of her destination and allowing events and memories to control her. Some words we could use to describe Janet include: pessimist, can't do, victim, complaining, making excuses, and as having a negative attitude.

Deep down, though, Janet knows she's taking the easy way out, because telling this story means she doesn't have to take responsibility for her life.

On the other hand, **Marie** stopped at the same time and is starting to move on to have a fulfilling life. She knows that she can't control *the* world but she can control *her* world and her reaction to it. She went through tough times and is now taking responsibility for her story and her life, and is driving her car where she wants it to go.

Marie knows that she did her best to have children; she went through the grieving process and now is starting to feel better. She also knows that not succeeding in one area of her life doesn't mean that she can't succeed elsewhere. She actively chooses to take responsibility for her results and feelings, and she knows that no one can ever 'make' her do or feel anything. She can be heard saying phrases like 'even though (… has happened), I can choose (how I want to feel, and how I move forward).'

Marie is in charge of her mind and what she says, does and feels, and therefore how she reacts to any situation, good or bad. Words we could use to describe her include: gets results, has a 'can do' and positive attitude, confidence, and belief.

Marie did this by changing the story she told herself. She'd had enough of being a victim and made a conscious decision to change the story she was telling herself. It wasn't like flicking a switch, it took some time and practice.

Do you recognise yourself in either of these stories? Are you a pessimistic Janet or are you starting to be a more optimistic Marie?

Why change?

The facts are the facts, but changing the story will change how you feel about not having children and how you feel about yourself. Being an optimist will help you to move on. If you want to stay stuck, being a pessimist and a victim is the best way I know. In many ways being the victim is comfortable because you don't have to face the future; you can stay here for as long as you like. Is that what you want? Really? Do you want to look back in five or ten years with regrets or would you prefer to do something now to change that?

If you're still not sure, spend a few moments considering what's keeping you stuck and the story you are telling yourself. Asking yourself the two questions below will help to uncover your reasons:

- What could you lose if you stop being a victim and are open to moving forward with your life?

- This will uncover the payoffs or secondary gain for you in staying stuck. It is important to think about your answer carefully.

- And what could you gain if you stop being a victim?

  I'll take a bet that these outweigh the payoffs.

If you still want to stay as a victim, I want to write that I understand. But I'm sorry, I can't. Being a victim is easier because it means you stay as you are. But you are missing out on *so much*.

When I hear childless women say things like 'I know I'm going to feel like this forever.' I want to shout 'no you don't, you absolutely don't.' I understand that you might be nervous about changing, but believe me, the rewards are worth it. If you're still unsure, please don't put this book down yet. Instead, read the next chapter. In it you'll read stories about what might lie ahead for you.

Your style has been with you since childhood so it's going to take time and commitment to change. Think of being in a car that is driving in deep ruts in the road, it will take some effort to steer out and take a different path. For some time it will fall back in, but then after a while, as it gains ground, it will start making new tracks.

My Story: From A Spelling Mistake to I Should Give Up My Business

I've never thought of myself as a victim in terms of my childlessness, but I do have a tendency to blow things out of proportion in my head. I'm not great with detail and if you follow me on social media you might notice that I make the odd spelling mistake. As soon as I notice it, I go into full catastrophizing mode. The voice is my head starts telling me I'm not good enough and, if I can't get simple spelling right, how on earth can I run a business, so I might as well give up now.

I can be like this in other areas too, especially if I have a misunderstanding with someone I care about. In a few seconds in my head I go from, we're great friends to she/he doesn't care about me anymore. I can spend anything from a few minutes to a couple of days in this space until I remember this quote from Viktor E. Frankl: *Between stimulus and response there is a space. In that space is our power to choose our response. In our response lies our growth and our freedom.*

It reminds me that I am in control of my thoughts and can decide my response, and this is just a story I'm telling myself and I can change it. Once I remember these things, I become calmer and more in control. Sometimes I let go of whatever was at the root of it, and other times I change the story. I'm still a work in progress, and I now remember more times than I forget.

Journaling Questions – Changing the Story

Think about Frankl's quote for a moment. There are spaces between your thoughts and also before you respond when someone speaks to you. I invite you to notice them, own them and expand them so you can frame your response in an empowering way.

This is a patient, step-by-step process; when you first start you may forget more times than you remember. What is important is to keep practising until it becomes a habit. Here's the best way to start:

- Start by noticing when you use pessimistic or victim words or phrases.

- Identify and label them.

- Label the phrase as 'this is a pessimistic thought'.

- Breathe. Take a breath into the space.

- Let the thought pass by.

- Before you respond, maybe count to three or four. Notice that space, own it, occupy it and use it to benefit you.

When you do this, you'll find that your mood will start to change and instead of disappearing down the rabbit hole of pessimism you'll have enough space and mental distance to consider a more optimistic story. You will read more about this and learn an exercise in Chapter Seven on Letting Go.

I have previously used the word 'victor' to describe the opposite of 'victim' but I don't believe that will resonate with you. I and some of my friends prefer to think of ourselves as female warriors. We are grounded, courageous, confident, living in accordance with our values, knowing that when we fall we have the tools to get back up. And mostly we are warriors with soft, open-hearted female strength, who choose love above everything else.

- I invite you to choose a word that resonates with you, maybe optimistic, warrior or victor, or something different. Get creative with it, and add some words or images of what she represents on a sheet of paper.

Chapter Five
If You Can Dream It, You Can Do It

If you can't dream it, you can't do it.

Martha Beck

Martha Beck is the author of *Finding Your Own North Star: How to Claim the Life You Were Meant to Live.* I chose this quote because she says that when her clients can't imagine doing something, it's genuinely impossible for them. And the opposite is also true.

Maybe until now, you didn't think you could have a fulfilling life without children, perhaps in part because you don't know anyone who is happy. Here's a slightly different angle from Marian Wright Edelman: *'you can't be what you can't see.'* So I'm here to show you, through examples of real women just like you, that you can.

My Story: Muddling Along Until I Found Role Models

When we finished IVF there were far fewer resources than there are now. I'm not a big fan of forums, meeting face to face is what helps me best. I met some wonderful women through More To Life and some of them have become my closest friends; however we were all at a similar stage in our healing journey so there was no one to look to as a mentor or guide. Sometimes we would play the 'name the childless woman' game and our answers would include women like Helen Mirren, Dolly Parton and the like. It was all very well to see famous women, but really, what do I have in common with them?

Then I found Pamela Mahoney Tsigdinos, Lisa Manterfield and Tracey Cleantis. When I read Pamela and Lisa's books I found women like me who were open and honest about what they'd been through and were now writing about 'life after' being childless. Reading their stories showed me that I wasn't alone and, more importantly that it is possible to be happy.

I believe in Martha's words completely: *If you can't dream it, you can't do it.* I'd been thinking about writing a book for a while, and I've already written that I had a really strong vision of holding it. At the same time there was a surge of power and strength through my body, coupled with an inner knowing that this is what I am *meant* to do. It was like flicking a switch. I dreamed it and immediately I knew I could do it.

I held on to this dream over the months of challenges I've faced to make it a reality. Two things encourage me to stay true to it. One is that I can see and feel it and, as I've already written, it is completely aligned with my values and who I am. Something inside me said, now is the time. You *must* do it.

When I say this was profound, I believe you know what I mean. Because by now, maybe your eyes are slightly open to the possibility that you could have a great life too. If you're not quite convinced, here's a taster of what some of our storytellers say about their life now.

Johanna Walker. I am stronger and healthier and sexier and more awake than ever before. My body is amazing. And I love what I can do with it. I can dance, hike, hug, run, walk, bike, listen, wait and watch, have sex and sweat, speak and perform, and take the stage and change the world. Thank Goddess for bodies.

Jessica Hepburn. I thank whoever for that blessing that life gave me in return for the thing it didn't give me. I just want women (and men) to go out and find what their blessings are. They won't be the same as mine but they are out there for the grabbing.

Helen Rebello. The biggest gift is how much time I get to spend with my husband and how lucky we are to embrace a life that's focused on doing what we want to do, travelling and exploring different things. We have changed our lives around. We had such a different life, this has given us freedom to explore completely new avenues and we are very different people now.

Emily Jacob. I have a very different kind of life than I would have had. And it's a really good life.

Rosalind Bubb. So now my life is happy and simple. I continue to be joyfully married and I love my work.

Tracey Cleantis. I had an absolute belief that I could not be happy without children and when it didn't happen, I was devastated with grief but it's been extraordinary to be so wrong.

August. My passion is my future, and making the absolute most of it I possibly can.

Louise. I can do what I like, when I like, with whom I like.

Liz Ashram. If I'd have had children, I wouldn't have started to teach Spanish and, subsequently, set up my own small business, which I love.

Did those words inspire you?

And are you slightly more open to the possibility that you could have this too?

Are you ready? Let's dream your future.

Set aside a few minutes in a quiet place to work through this. If you'd prefer to listen you can also download it.

Sit quietly, feel your feet on the floor and your body where it touches the chair.

Breathe in gently to the count of four, and out to the count of four. Do that a few times and feel your body relax.

Imagine you're walking in a wood, and you come across the junction of two possible ways forward. One is where your life stayed the same as it is now, and the other is where you did what you needed to live a fulfilling life.

Imagine taking the first. Take yourself down the path to maybe a year, two, five years ahead; you stayed feeling as you are now. You are still in the cocoon feeling exactly as you are now, or maybe sadder and more alone than now, because you know you had a golden opportunity and you didn't take it. Imagine all of it. What do you see, hear, and feel. What are others saying to you and what are you saying to yourself?

Take it all in and notice how heavy it feels in your body.

Now come back to the crossroads. Shake it all off (if it helps, get up and shake your arms and legs).

Now let's imagine taking the second path. Walk to a year, two, five years ahead. You did what you needed to do and now you are living as that beautiful butterfly in the world. You are comfortable in your own skin and confident talking about your life. How would that be? Imagine all the possibilities. What do you see, hear, and feel? What are others saying to you and what are you saying to yourself?

Take it all in and notice how different it feels in your body, how you feel so much lighter.

Once you've absorbed it all, come back to the crossroads

Open your eyes and come back to now.

Now ask yourself, which life do you want?

Do you want the first, staying in the cocoon? If you do, that's your choice and I'm very sorry. And what if, instead of putting this book away, you were to stay curious and leave it out somewhere obvious? I'm a believer in fate; so why not open it from time to time, you never know, something might catch your eye and change your mind.

If you're ready to move on and explore the changes, let me take you by the hand and lead you gently through Act Two where you'll discover the beautiful butterfly inside you that is waiting to emerge.

As you work through the chapters and questions in Act Two, keep an eye on your values. They will guide you to take the action that steers you towards the authentic you.

A final word – what might pull you away and what will help you stay?

Do you ever commit to something fully intending to see it through, maybe even believing you'll enjoy it? And then part way through you suddenly realise it's harder than you thought and you want to stop? This happens to me every time I go to a more energetic yoga class, and my thought process goes like this.

I love yoga and I love this class – I want to be fitter and this will help me - I can do it – it's hard but I can do it – No wait, this is really hard – I'm not sure I can do it - Why am I doing it? – How much longer is there to go? – Exactly why am I doing this? – I know I said I want to do it, but now I'm not sure - I hate yoga – No, I really hate yoga and this class – I never want to do this class again - Ah now I feel the benefits – I'm enjoying it and I can do it – Now I've got over the hard bit I realise it's not as difficult as I thought it would be - I love yoga and I love this class – Where can I sign up for the next one?

Is that familiar?

I believe that this is how the change process works. The caterpillar has to go through many challenges to become a butterfly.

There are two pieces of self-awareness that will help you. They are the answers to these questions – what might stop you, and what will help you to keep going.

What might pull you away?

What do you usually do when things get hard? Do you keep going or do you (like most of us at some point) have avoidance strategies? These are things you do to distract yourself from the task at hand and to avoid challenges. It is often called numbing because it's something we do to temporarily avoid or numb the pain. However, as you'll read later, pain is the agent of change and the behaviors you use to avoid it can cause more harm than facing it.

Examples of these avoidance strategies could be social media, food, drink, or shopping. For example I am really good at distracting myself with social media when writing gets hard. When I feel challenging emotions such as anxiety or stress, instead of leaning in to them, I may eat a whole bar of chocolate instead. I then eat it quickly, I don't enjoy it and I feel bad afterwards.

And what will help you stay?

There are also those things that will encourage you to stay the course, to lean in to the challenges that you will encounter in Act Two. Here are four suggestions:

1. Reconnect with the vision you created above. Keep reminding yourself that you *can* have a fulfilling life without children, and that you really want it. Keep that to hand, and remember that you can always re-read the stories from time to time.

2. Now that you've worked out your values, reminding yourself that what you're doing is true to them will also help.

3. There are small things that nourish you which you can use to stay on course. On the wall behind my desk I have a list of what I call *small pleasures*: things I can do that bring me joy and steer me back on course. Most of them are free, such a pausing to look up at the sky, a hug from Roger, meditating, reading, looking at photos, singing along to a favourite song ,or a long bath. Others cost a small amount, such as one square of chocolate, coffee in my favourite mug, a yoga class, or buying a bunch of flowers.

   These days I'm better at noticing when I'm getting pulled away or distracted and I do one of these to re-connect me and give me a pause and reset. They make my day more fun and pleasurable and remind me that my aim is to enjoy writing, not make it punitive.

4. And there are bigger things too, which centre you, or connect you to your source, your roots, who you are or maybe who you used to be.

   Think about a tree, having strong roots holds it straight and gives it the firmness and connection to the ground and its surroundings. They hold it up. It may sway in the winds, but if the roots are strong it won't fall over. They also give it a sense of permanence. The stronger its roots, the taller and stronger it can grow. So it is with you. If you get rocked about, connecting to what makes you feel stable will give you a sense of solidity and steadiness and give you the courage to grow further. Examples of this could be your spirituality or faith or your connection to a particular place.

My Story: Connecting to My Roots

When I'm challenged several things that bring me back are my Christian faith, The Yorkshire Dales and spending time on the yoga mat.

My Christian faith isn't a massive part of my life but it is important, especially when I'm thrown off course. It anchors me to something solid, something I believe in. Attending a service or simply entering a church makes me feel peaceful and grounded. I especially appreciate Church of England churches that are hundreds of years old. . I often think about the number of people who have worshipped there, who've shared their struggles in this place, before God. I particularly like the church where my parents' funerals were held. The Vicar and congregation are friendly, and I get a wonderful connection and sense of belonging. The connection I feel is to something bigger and solid that hasn't changed for many years, which was there before me and will continue afterwards.

I get that connection to source also on the yoga mat and when I get outside into the countryside, especially my beloved Yorkshire Dales. There is something about those green fields, limestone walls, and open skies that are very special to me. I love to stand and pause, take a few deep breaths and feel the stillness and connection deep within me. After a church service, a yoga lesson, or a walk in the countryside I am refreshed and renewed, ready to start again.

These are bigger sources of inspiration that bring me back to me and remind me why I'm doing this work and you will have those, too.

Journaling Questions

Before you start Act Two, ask yourself:

- What behaviour is likely to pull me away?

- What do I usually do when things get hard?

- What do I usually do to numb those challenging feelings?

- What do I do to distract myself?

- What can I do to help me stay the course?

- How can I stay connected to the life I want?

- How can I remind myself of my values?

- What small things (small pleasures) can I do to keep me on course?

- And what are the bigger things which connect me to my roots/source/me?

Having an awareness of these things will help you to keep going.

Act Two

Finding Your Wings

Introduction

Just when the caterpillar thought the world was over, she became a butterfly.

Barbara Haines Howett,
from Ladies of the Borobudur

It's now time to do the work of transformation. It might be messy and you might want to quit, but the main thing is to keep moving a step at a time. Small steps will take you a long way.

At times you may think that nothing is happening, that it's dark and never ending. But a caterpillar has to be unmade before it becomes a butterfly. At this stage, you don't know what colour and shape your wings will be. Working this out will take time.

Remember the supplies you gathered in Act One (your Wheel of Life, your values, the techniques you've earned to change your mindset, and your visualisation), and keep them close by. They will guide your way.

The first chapter I wrote in Act Two was about grief. When I finished I thought, yes, job done. I now realise that the whole of Act Two is about moving through the grieving process. Each chapter is a slightly different way of doing so and they are linked. Some will appeal to you and some won't, and that's okay.

The key to the whole book is to read with a curious mind and be open to the possibility that it could help you.

Chapter Six
To Grieve, Or Not To Grieve?
You Know The Answer

Grief is the price we pay for love.

Queen Elizabeth II

Okay, I'll dive straight in and say it out loud: *You are grieving.*

I know you probably don't want to hear this, but you are.

In grief, *anything* and *everything* is 'normal'. There is no 'normal' way to be. And while our experiences and expressions of grief are as unique as we are, there is only one rule:

You must go through it.

I'm sorry, I'm guessing you probably didn't want to hear that either.

Grief is probably the emotion we most fear. We're afraid of the darkness it brings and the expectations society has on us about dealing with it. You can pretend it isn't happening and you might get away with ignoring it for a while, but in the end it will rear its fangs and bite you. The words said by Queen Elizabeth II after 9/11 put a lovely spin on things, but they don't make the work of grieving any easier.

I'm guessing that your family and friends might not have known you were trying for children, so they won't know that you're grieving. And even if they do know, they probably won't understand. So, unless you know other women in the same situation, or have really understanding friends, I'm sorry to say that you're on your own.

I'm also guessing you've been grieving for a while now. You may have been trying to avoid it or have not labelled it as grief. Perhaps you've been angry or you feel sad all the time, fed up, listless, and unmotivated. Maybe you've been snapping at your friends or partner. We all work through it differently, and I'd like to offer you some stories, from myself and others, on how we approached grieving. As with each chapter, I hope you'll see yourself in one or more of these stories and find some guidance and comfort.

My Story: Pull Yourself Together And Carry On (or How Not To Do It)

My whole life I've followed the pattern of not showing my feelings, living by the mantra 'pull yourself together and carry on.'

I grew up in Yorkshire in northern England. For readers unfamiliar with this part of the world, we are known for saying what we mean (some might call it blunt), and, as for speaking about our feelings, we don't do that.

My parents taught me many wonderful things, but not how to express how I felt. I loved my dad dearly, and he was a rock. He bore everything life threw at him with the stoicism of that generation who lived through the Second World War. He'd been through so much grief in his life (losing both parents before he was 13, then becoming partially sighted when he was in his 50s) and in the 52 years I knew him, he cried only once in my presence. When I was seven Mum bought us a surprise holiday to Norway, and he was so moved by the gesture, he left the room to hide his emotions. I didn't see him cry when Mum died or when he was told (out of the blue) that he had terminal cancer.

When I was ten, my parents had an allotment near the playground. One day, when I was playing on the swings, I fell and banged my head and I didn't cry because there were people around. Instead, I got up, walked (or maybe ran) to my parents, and allowed myself to cry for only a few moments as Mum soothed me, telling me not to cry.

Over time I developed this into a new skill. Each time I felt like I was about to cry I took those feelings out of my head, put them in a box, and closed the lid. Job done. I promised myself that I'd take them out later but guess what? Over time I piled more into the box and kept forcing down the lid.

When we went through IVF, this was my pattern of behaviour. I remember our last round. When I started to bleed I was absolutely devastated, knowing that we would never have our own child. But I didn't allow myself to cry. I was at work and couldn't fall apart. I held on until Roger picked me up from the station. I cried for the ten minutes it took us to drive home, then made myself stop. The next day, I was back at work, emotions all in check, and no one knew anything had happened. Outside I was the same, and outside I stayed the same for many years. Looking back I now realise I was grieving, but at the time I was just sad and numb.

Four years later, when Mum was terminally ill and I was staying in the house with her and Dad, I remember willing myself not to cry and hiding my head under the bedclothes as I didn't want Dad to hear me crying. Another time, just before she died, I started crying as Roger and I drove away from the house and forced myself to stop 30 minutes later when we pulled in for petrol.

I didn't cry when she died or at her funeral. I felt numb and every time anything bubbled up, it went into the box. After all, Dad was keeping everything inside, so I felt that I should too.

Then, a few years later, my dad died. The only time I cried was the day before his funeral when the Vicar called to ask if I was okay, and then it was only for a moment. Being an only child there was a lot to do to arrange his funeral and organise his affairs so I was busy and by now, not showing my emotions was the only thing I knew how to do. I also wanted to make my parents proud by doing what they taught me, by not *feeling* but *doing*.

I believed I could outrun grief and if you'd asked me at the time, my beliefs about it were something like this:

- Grief is an enemy that must be kept at arm's length.

- I must armour up, because if grief gets too close, I'll fall apart.

- I can't fall apart.

- If I ignore grief, it will go away.

- I must bury my feelings.

- Feeling is bad.

- Time is a healer. If I keep doing all the above, the grief will pass.

For thirteen years after we finished IVF I kept stuffing everything I didn't want to feel into that box. From time to time, the lid came off at unexpected and inopportune moments: I got over emotional at funerals, I'd snap at Roger out of the blue, I felt sad and listless, and I regularly burst into tears. In the early days I could manage myself, but after many years the box got so full that the lid just wouldn't stay closed. On the outside and to most of my friends I was the confident, capable Lesley that they all knew. Inside, however, I was falling apart. And believe me, I tried *really hard* to ignore what was happening because as far as I was concerned, I had pulled myself together and carried on.

People who loved me told me grief was not an enemy but a friend. They told me lovingly that I couldn't outrun it forever; I would have to take my armour off at some point and there was magic in doing so. I resisted big time until I finally realised my beliefs about grief were just stories I was telling myself. They weren't my stories. Rather, they were stories I'd learned from my parents, and I could change them.

But how?

A solution appeared through an invite to a workshop based on Brené Brown's book *Rising Strong*. I travelled to Las Vegas, and learned—in my 50s—that feelings are called feelings because you actually *feel* them in your body. It's not that I hadn't felt things before, it was simply the first time I connected what happened in my *body* with what was going on in my *head*.

It was also the first time in my life that I cried openly and freely, and oh my goodness did I do a lot of it that weekend! I also shattered those unhelpful and unhealthy beliefs I'd been carrying around for so many years. My new beliefs included:

- Keeping busy and not feeling is the worst thing to do.

- Grief will eventually find its way out.

- As the saying goes, 'It's better out than in!', so when emotion comes up, feel it and let it go. It will pass.

- Time is a healer to some extent, and healing happens much quicker if you do the grief work.

- Expressing your feelings is a sign of strength.

Everything has changed for me since that workshop. I've learned how different emotions feel in my body. I name sensations as I feel them; for example, tingling, numbness, heat, tension. And I'm comfortable showing them on the outside too.

I've also changed my self-talk when something bubbles up to the surface. I now welcome feelings and say to myself, 'Ah something else is coming up for healing.' If I can name it, I do so. I remind myself that it's just a memory; I've been here before, I lived through the event, and I can live through this. I don't question what's behind it. Many times I have no idea, and it doesn't matter; I lean in to it, feel it, and know that it will pass.

I'm also gentle with myself, I understand that a habit I've had for over 50 years won't change overnight. So when I feel myself suppressing emotions, I remind myself that *'Tears are the rain of life and nothing grows without water.'* (Unknown)

When I look back, I believe that my grieving took place at a time when I was open to asking for help and undergoing the transformation that happened as a result. And perhaps I needed to be strong enough, too. Maybe I wasn't ready earlier. Perhaps I wouldn't have been able to arrange Dad's funeral if I hadn't been so strong and focused. I'll never know.

The main thing I have learned is that running from grief doesn't work. It will eventually catch you, maybe when you least expect it, so it's better to face it in your own time and your own way.

Lisa Manterfield's story is similar to mine, which is hardly surprising as our roots are both in Yorkshire.

I was so entrenched in having a baby, and I wasn't given the tools to deal with grief. I didn't understand that childlessness was a loss, a big loss, to your identity, as well as your place in the family, in your social network, and among friends. It took me a long time to understand it was a loss I needed to grieve.

There are many social expectations around death, and one is that after six months you'll be over it. The first year of losing someone is just a mess. You don't know which way is up, let alone begin grieving. Just about the time you start your grieving is the time everyone thinks you're over it.

It kept creeping out. I burst into tears in the office after a call; I snapped at my husband and got upset at really trivial things. It was a gradual realisation over time, and when I read about the five stages of grief that Elizabeth Kubler Ross writes about, I said to myself, 'Oh, oh, that's what this is.'

I'd love to say that I had a great realisation and then swung into action, but that would be a lie. I didn't do a lot of the things I recommend (get help, find a support group or therapist), but I did write. A lot.

The identity that you're never going to have is a massive loss and has to be dealt with, worked through around and across, to come out the other side.

It's been eight years since we decided that was it. And, as the saying goes, 'You've come a long way baby.' Now I can be around children, and I can talk openly about it; lots of things don't upset me anymore.

But I don't think it ever goes away, I don't think you ever get over it. I think it's always going to be part of who you are. It becomes a smaller and smaller part and you learn to live around it. In the early days it is everything, all encompassing. Anything that anyone says to you, you filter it through this loss, this thing you don't have. It gets better with time, and you really have to deal with it; at some point, it's going to be unpleasant, messy.

My words of wisdom are 'Be kind to yourself.' Lots of people don't understand. You may not get the kindness and compassion from others that you'd really like, so you have to give it to yourself.

> At some point you have to sit down and face it, however that is. It will find a way out eventually, so you might as well find a healthy outlet and deal with it.

Tracey Cleantis shared her wisdom about grieving from both her personal and professional perspectives.

> As a therapist, I knew the consequences of not grieving. I'm a person who feels deeply. I knew it was a significant investment, a significant dream. Grief is not just about death. It's about loss of different stages in life, identity, loss of who you might have been, all of the other unprocessed identities.
>
> With so much hurt in my life, I knew I couldn't just move on to the next thing. Intuitively I knew that I needed to give space to that and simultaneously I got a lot of messages from friends and family saying, 'You've got to move on', 'You've got to look on the bright side', 'Get back on the horse again!' And our culture says to us, 'It's too much,' 'Aren't you done with this by now?', 'You've had your minute; Time to move on!'
>
> When I finally decided 'No more,' I let out an animal cry I'd never heard from myself before. It was a keening full-body grief. It's important for our relationships to be able to say to our friends, 'This is where I am. I'm going to be here for a while. Can you be here with me?' If they can't, find a group, find a therapist, find places where there's just space to feel that raw, unedited feeling.
>
> When I could no longer talk to friends and family, I knew that I needed to get into therapy so that I would have a space where I could just unapologetically grieve. As Brené Brown says, it's about finding that safe person to share with.

If you don't intuitively know how to grieve, there are things you can do to connect you to that grief. Try writing a letter to that longed-for child, or writing a letter to that self you imagined, that life you imagined. Flesh it out and let the feelings flow. You might also look for online communities of other women, a safe place with people who get you, where you can be honest about your feelings and you don't have to bottle anything up.

The other piece is that if you don't do this, it will have consequences. It will affect your ability to be happy, to really engage with life. The truth is grief is like an anaesthetic. It's not, 'this is the infertility piece: I'm going to numb that.' Everything else will be affected too. When you numb, you numb. As Brené Brown says, 'When you numb the dark, you numb the light.'

And acceptance doesn't mean that grief won't circle around. You revisit it, from different angles. You're never going to be in that same place again, but you will revisit it. So view the grieving process as an opportunity to be responsive to yourself. Give yourself space for those feelings.

And from **Jody Day.**

Grief, however heavy it might feel, is not actually the problem – it's the solution, the way out, the way through. Learn as much as you can about grief and make friends with it. Find out what it wants of you, and cooperate with it (even though it's the last thing you want to do). Grief doesn't have to be a life-sentence of misery, but avoiding grief can keep you stuck for years. Time does not heal grief, only grieving does.

I have come to understand grief as a form of love and, like love, it needs to be 'in relationship'. Many of us are experiencing our grief in isolation, in our heads, alone in our rooms and lives, and that's not how grief heals – it heals by being in relationship, in dialogue with others who totally 'get it' – because grief is a dialogue not a monologue. It is a social emotion so you need to find others to accompany you through this passage.

What did you learn from Lisa, Tracey, and Jody?

For me, they reinforce what it took me a long time to learn; that you can't outrun grief. And also how important it is to find a safe space to be yourself, whether that's with a therapist or in a group.

If you're not grieving, what are you doing instead?

Let's go back to what Tracey was saying and the quote she mentioned from Brené Brown *'when you numb the dark, you numb the light.'* What she means is that when you decide not to feel grief, sadness, disappointment – all those dark emotions – you will also miss out on the light emotions such as joy and happiness.

In Act One I asked you to make a list of those things you use to numb, so go back and remind yourself of what you wrote. If necessary, add to it. The key is to be aware of where and when you're numbing.

To Grieve You Need To Feel

And now for **Helen Rebello's** story.

100

Grieving is not easy but if I can do it anyone can. I was brought up to not express my feelings and hide behind a veil of humour. I got really good at doing that, putting a veneer on. It took me a long time to learn how to get in touch with and to access my feelings.

I realised that things I wasn't expressing were starting to come out in overt ways. That's the first clue. For instance, if I've said something that's not really like me.

I was already dabbling with yoga. I'd approached it as something to give me some space. Something within me said 'yoga is the way' and I started to spend more time with myself, with my body, doing my yoga practice and being more in my own space and less concerned with what other people were doing around me.

Then I started to notice all the things I was feeling and I started finding ways to express them in very safe spaces, mostly with my husband.

I had a multi-pronged approach: yoga, writing, and not holding back.

Over time I got better at being able to be okay with the different things that came up as I recognised that they would come and go.

I realised that this was the route to access all the positive. You can't have one without the other and you're not fully experiencing your life if you don't allow yourself to experience them all.

I also realised that nobody else is going to get you out of this; the only person who can rescue you is you.

By now I hope you are starting to accept that, as the heading says, to grieve you need to feel emotions as they arise.

Mindfulness – one way in to feeling.

In her story, **August** found mindfulness to be a really helpful way to open up her feelings. Here's her experience.

My 40th birthday didn't go so well. It felt like a big line was finally being drawn under the whole 'able to have children' thing. I refused to celebrate – what was there to celebrate? I sank back into depression and one of the things my doctor offered was an 8-week course in Mindfulness Based Stress Reduction (MBSR).

Learning how to apply mindfulness in my daily life was revelatory. I suddenly understood that the negative scripts and destructive rumination that played out across my mind were not, in fact, reality at all, and I did not have to be defined by them. In turn, learning how to meditate and to try and calm these tormenting thoughts when they arose was a gift – one that needs to be cultivated for sure, but one that has thankfully made me more resilient and less likely to fall back into the clutches of depression.

In one of my favourite mindful meditations by Jon Kabat-Zinn (the founder of MBSR and author of the classic text on the subject *Wherever You Go, There You Are*) he suggests that we might imagine our emotions, thoughts and feelings as a body of water that flows past us like a river. We can watch their flow and gently observe their course without throwing ourselves bodily into the water.

This proved to be a very helpful concept for me. It helped me understand that, on any given day (depending on where I am emotionally), that body of water may a babbling brook, a swaying ocean, an incessant waterfall, a violent torrent – and I have choices to make about how I want to engage with this water. I can, if I wish, sit on the shore and observe it flowing, or I can dive right in and get wet. As a bystander, an observer, I can watch the waters pass by, ebb and flow, as they always will. And, like bodies of water, sometimes my thoughts and emotions rage, and when raging, only a fool would dive in and try to swim.

Over time, and with practice, I have learned that it is possible to sit by the river and watch my thoughts and emotions pass. To be present with them at that moment but not necessarily get dragged into them.

I also sometimes find it helpful to consider some of my more difficult thoughts and feelings as entities in their own right – creatures that I recognise and speak to with understanding and compassion – a technique I learned from my very favourite book on the subject by Paul Gilbert and Chodron entitled *Mindful Compassion – Using the Power of Mindfulness and Compassion to Transform Our Lives*.

Through my reading, and the practicing of these ideas and exercises, I have learned how to be kinder and more forgiving toward myself. Because I am human, some days it works better than others. Being mindful means being aware of the here and now, and not being caught up in endless rumination about the past or constantly worrying about what may or may not happen in the future.

Awareness means remembering to be present, in the reality of this moment I have in my hands. It also means remembering not to berate myself when I don't do that so well – it is the everyday trying that counts, and the recognition and correction when I catch myself veering off course.

Mindfulness has helped me to catch myself when I get caught up in this negative self-flagellation and remember that I (just like everyone else) am simply trying to do my best from day to day, and that is all we can ever ask of ourselves and of each other.

I really connect with what August says. Working through Jon Kabat-Zinn's 8-week MBSR course started me on the mindfulness path and also lead me to yoga which I absolutely love and has changed my life in many ways.

To grieve, you need to feel emotions as they arise. If you're not used to it this, it can be a challenge. For me, the key is mindfulness, which is really being aware of the moment, having a courageous presence. The next time you feel grief rear its head, maybe sit or lie somewhere quietly and follow these steps:

- *Close your eyes.*
- *Ask yourself: what is happening inside me now, where do I feel it in my body, what am I thinking now? How can I describe it? For example, is it tingling, numbing or heat?*
- *Just notice and be aware. There is no judgement.*

- *Naming sensations can reduce their intensity, so name your feeling if you can. Maybe you will recall having felt this before, or maybe it is new. Whatever and however it feels, it is perfect. If you want to cry, do so.*

- *Be present, focus on the moment and notice how it changes as it moves, peaks and then dissipates.*

- *Remember to breathe, I know that sounds obvious but in stressful times you may hold your breath. You can use your breath as an anchor, focusing on it consciously. Maybe breathe in and out to a count of three or four, noticing where you feel it in your body. You could say to yourself 'I'm breathing in' and' I'm breathing out' as you count, or 'let it go, let it go' or my favourite is to say 'calm' as I breathe in and 'ease' as I breathe out.*

- *As the feelings dissipate, end with a moment of gratitude. Ask yourself, 'what are three things I'm grateful for in this moment?'*

After a while you'll start to recognise each feeling as it comes up and learn to *have* them and not be hijacked by them. I remember when I was in the workshop in Vegas, we were talking about grief and as it was due to be my turn I felt a real tension in the top of my head and I wanted to flee. In the past I thought this was the start of a headache and now I realise it's anxiety. When I feel it now, instead of reaching for the painkillers or numbing it with chocolate, I realise I'm anxious and take action to soothe and calm myself.

You don't have to suffer.

There's also plenty of evidence that you don't have to suffer. Shinzen Young, a well-respected American meditation teacher, proposed that pain is inevitable but suffering is not. He says that the relationship between pain and suffering can be expressed through this equation:

Suffering = Pain x Resistance.

Suffering, Young suggests, comes from resisting pain and of course the more we resist what's happening, the more we suffer. He says that suffering is the mental anguish caused by fighting against the fact that life is painful. You can't avoid pain in life; however, you don't have to suffer because of it.

Others have a similar view. In *The Wise Heart: A Guide to the Universal Teachings of Buddhist Psychology*, Jack Kornfield writes that suffering is our reaction to the inevitable pain of life and it can include things such as anxiety, depression, fear, confusion, grief, anger, and hurt. He quotes the sixteenth principle of Buddhist psychology as *'Pain is inevitable. Suffering is not. Suffering arises from grasping. Release grasping and be free of suffering.'*

I understand that. Do you?

I can see that emotional suffering is caused by wanting life to be different from how it is and the more you resist how life actually is, the more you suffer. I think you know this already. Not being able to have children is extremely painful, and you can't change it. By resisting and not accepting it, you're suffering more than you need to.

Part of the grieving process is about accepting what is and letting go of what cannot be. We'll talk more about letting go in the next chapter.

I hope you've read enough now to realise *that you have to go into the pain.* I would say, get curious about the pain, don't be afraid of it; be afraid of what you do to distract yourself from feeling.

Another way to look at grief.

In *Rising Strong*, Brené Brown describes three elements of grief that emerged from her research. They were loss, longing, and feeling lost. For you these could translate this way:

Loss. You've lost an identity and the life you thought you'd have, a future self that now isn't going to exist. This loss has to be honoured and given time and attention.

Longing. She describes this as an *involuntary yearning for wholeness, for meaning.* You know this well because it comes out of nowhere and crashes over you like a wave every time you see someone who's pregnant or a work colleague brings in their scan. It's that feeling when you see a mother with her children and with all your heart you long to change places with her.

Feeling lost. This is the need to reorient yourself to your world and is described in terms such as feeling frozen or losing your bearings.

When you put these three together it's no wonder that you're struggling. And when you throw in the fact that those around you don't understand what you've lost, it's even harder.

Looking back I realise that I've felt all of these. For a while, the feelings of no longer being a daughter were really strong, and when you add being an only child to that, it was almost like my early life didn't happen because there's now no one else who shared the happy times I had, especially with my parents. This made me feel lost, like I was bobbing around on the sea without an anchor. My task, then, was to find the anchor within myself and as you read on, you'll learn how I did this and found my joy again.

To finish with a story.

When my mum died the Vicar explained that in his view, grief is like putting on a rucksack at the start of a long walk. It feels heavy in the beginning, and the longer you carry it the lighter it feels. There will be times when you'll even forget that you're carrying it because it's so light and other times when the weight of it will seem to crush you.

In my experience—and that of the storytellers—this is true. The rucksack that carries our childless grief is now light and we mostly forget that we're carrying it. Even if now and again we feel a slight tug, these times are fewer in number and don't crush us anymore.

Journaling Questions

- What are the key things you've learned from this chapter? Which areas would be helpful for you to explore? Examine these as you write in your journal.

  I hope I've convinced you that you can't outrun grief. You have to go through it at some point, so why not on your own terms? Here are some ways to start.

- If love were in the room, what would she say about what you've been doing until now and what would she advise you to do?

Let's examine your beliefs about grief by answering some or all of these questions:

- What are they? Write them down. Are they true?

- Whose beliefs are they really? Who gave them to you? When have they not been true for you or others? Who do you know who believes something different?

- Having read this and knowing what you know now, what would be useful to believe instead? Write these new beliefs down. And remember that you've changed beliefs before, many times. Think of something you used to believe (for example, The Tooth Fairy), could this be the same?

- Examine your feelings about loss, longing, and feeling lost. Write about these and how they show up in your life.

- Go back to the list you made in Act One of those things you do to stop feeling and the actions that bring you back. How do you use them to avoid feeling?

- Find a space where you can process your feelings, maybe with a therapist or a group, or by writing; a place where you can be completely honest and vulnerable.

- You could also carry out the exercises Tracey suggests such as writing a letter to that longed-for child, or writing a letter to that self you imagined, that life you imagined. Flesh it out and let the feelings flow.

Remember, your heart will show you the way if you make time and space to listen to it.

And above all, be patient and kind to yourself. Kindness is the way in.

Chapter Seven

Letting Go Or Letting In? You Decide

It takes a lot more courage to let something go than it does to hang on to it, trying to make it better.

Letting go doesn't mean ignoring a situation. Letting go means accepting what is, exactly as it is, without fear, resistance, or a struggle for control.

Iyanla Vanzant

Why You Must Let Go

I know you tried with all your heart and body to be a mother; however, holding on to any tiny dream you still have of it coming true is keeping you stuck. Your heart knows this. You're not yet sure what life is waiting for you, but trust me, you must first let go of the dream of motherhood and everything that goes with it, before you can move on to a new life.

For a caterpillar to transform it must first let go of its old life, as well as its dreams for that life. In your heart of hearts you know this is what you must do, especially as you are still feeling the emotional pain of being childless.

Make space to let more in.

I understand how tough this is, I'm asking you to let go of the dream that kept you going for many years. But what if, instead of thinking about letting go, you viewed this as making space to let in more dreams?

Yes I know, when I first heard this I wasn't sure either. I discussed it with my yoga teacher **Emma Peel.** Here's a summary of our conversation.

Letting go allows us to make room for more possibilities. When we let go of a particular version of how we think life should be we free ourselves to be open to new experiences and different ways of thinking. It's not a question of letting go of the dream; it's about opening yourself up to more dreams.

We should be aware of what we attach ourselves to, especially what we understand is 'good' and 'bad' and to be aware when we're focused on only one outcome. By letting go we let in many other options we may have never considered.

Think of a tree; it's not hanging on to its leaves for dear life. Instead it lets them fall as part of a process. The leaves fall; they go back into the earth to fertilise it and prepare it for new growth. It is the process. There is also a gap between the leaves falling and new growth and it's also key to be aware of and to take time to sit in that gap.

As we let go, we gain understanding. It's important to ask yourself: where did that dream or story come from, what do you feel it would have offered you, and can you realize it in another way? By doing this we're expanding the parameters of our life and our goals, and we're opening ourselves up to letting in many more possibilities.

> There is a fear that if we let go we can potentially lose a part of ourselves. But it is the opposite, because as we let go, we learn more about who we are and we also let more in that will enrich us.

I love this reframe to a far more positive concept of opening up and letting in, and you'll read in my story how letting go has let so much more into my life.

Think about it for a moment; when you were completely focused on wanting to be a mother, there was little room for anything else. I appreciate that was what you had to do for a while, especially if you were going through treatment. But it's time now to focus on other areas of your life. Perhaps areas you've never considered.

Trust me, there *is* something special waiting for you but it can't manifest because there's no room for it. As Emma said, the tree has to let go of its leaves before new ones can grow. It must first allow the leaves to fall and provide fertiliser to create more growth. It is the same for us. That life you wanted is keeping you from living fully, *right now*. If you want to move forward in your life you have to make room for new possibilities. Your past dreams and desires are taking up too much room and the new can't come in until you make space for it.

I'm going to labour this point by asking you several *big* questions.

1. **By the time you get to the end of this book do you want to have put behind the dreams of motherhood, the sadness**

and grief or do you still want to drag them behind you like a ball and chain?

Be honest. If the answer is you don't want to put it behind you, ask yourself why that is.

2. **What are you willing to give up, in order to have a new life?**

    Something you're doing—consciously or unconsciously—is keeping you where you are now. Are you willing to give that up? Are you willing to give up hiding, secrecy? Are you willing to give up being proud and ask for help?

    With both of these questions, if you're not yet convinced that you're ready, go deeper into the question and explore it in your writing. If, after writing, you're still unsure, I suggest you hold that for now and carry on reading with an open mind.

3. **What's stopping you from achieving your greatest potential?**

    In this stuck and unhappy place, you are not achieving everything you can in life, you also know that. Let's dig a bit deeper into what *is* stopping you.

What Are You Letting Go Of?

To quote Tracey Cleantis in our discussion about grieving, *'Grief is not just about death. It's about loss of different stages in life; identity, loss of who you might have been.'*

With every ending of a dream there has to be a letting go of both the identity you thought you'd have and the associated beliefs that go with it. When I was younger I dreamed of being a sports teacher. I imagined myself teaching in a girls' school just like the one I attended, where all the pupils were polite and loved sport (yes, I know it was a dream). Then my teachers told me bluntly that I wasn't good enough, and, if I wanted to play sport it was better to do it in my own time rather than teach. Logically, this made sense, but emotionally, I was devastated. After a while I realised they were right and, letting go of striving and the need to keep improving enabled me to relax and enjoy sport a lot more.

Of course, there is little comparison between letting go of that dream and letting go of your dream of being a mother but there is an important parallel. I had to let go of imagining myself as a teacher and living the life that went with it. That dream had to die for me to fully enjoy that aspect of my life. In her book *The Next Happy: Let Go of the Life You Planned and Find a New Way Forward*, Tracey Cleantis suggests that if you declare the 'Time of Death' for a dream, you will regain some control over your life. I'm guessing that you just recoiled in horror, but inside you know this is what you need to do. You know that the dream of being a mother is already dead and holding on to it is keeping you a caterpillar and holding you back from becoming the beautiful butterfly you are.

Let's explore what you'll be letting go of.

Three things to let go of.

There are three things to let go of: **emotions** as they arise, the **dreams** and hopes you had and any related **memorabilia** you're holding on to.

Emotions. I wrote in the previous chapter that to grieve you must feel emotions as they arise and then consciously let them go. If you skipped over that because it was too hard, I'm sorry but you need to go back.

Elizabeth Gilbert used the term 'museum to grief' in a Facebook post and it applies here. When you're hanging on to dreams, your house and mind can feel like a museum to grief. Ask yourself: How many times do you think about what might have been? How many times a (day or) week do you wish that you were a mother? How often do you walk through the museum of the negativity from your past, take something from the shelf, dust it off and think about it? It makes you feel worse, doesn't it?

It might seem comforting to think about what might have been, but it's holding you back. It's time to clear out every 'what might have been', every 'should have', every 'could have' and every 'I wish I had' from your past so you can move forward with positivity and confidence.

Memorabilia. You probably also have mementos in your museum. Perhaps you saved reminders of your hospital appointments, or you bought something you were going to give to your baby. Each and every time you take a look at these things you're stumbling over your past and stopping yourself from having the future you want. Clearing space in your house and your head will enable you to move forward.

You know how clear-headed and positive you feel when you clear out your wardrobe and make space for that new outfit? This is exactly the same.

Now it's time to go through your house and gather up all the evidence of wanting to be a mother. All of it. Put it to one side for a moment, read the stories below and then decide what sort of ceremony you'll have to let go of your museum.

Dreams. What we're discussing here is the need to let go of your dream of being a mother and letting go of that identity. And this was a *big dream*. Maybe you've had this dream ever since you got your first doll when you were five years old. Maybe it's a dream you always assumed you'd achieve. Perhaps this dream took on an even greater urgency when you met your partner. Whatever it is, now is the time to let it go.

I'd love to say that you can spin round three times and it will be gone, but we both know that's not the case. I'm also sorry to tell you that you'll have to let go of this time and time again. When you feel sad upon seeing a 'happy family' – let it go. When you feel regret when you see mothers at the school gates – let it go. When you experience anger when your friend becomes a grandmother – let it go.

This might not be easy, but it is absolutely worth it. If you're not sure that you even want to start, jump ahead and read Act Three and see what the storytellers have let into their lives now that they've let go of their museum to grief. They have their life now that they've let go.

How to let go.

Letting go of a feeling is about noticing it when it comes up; leaning in to it, feeling it, and then realising that it passes. That is to feel *everything in each moment* so you can let it go. And doing this over and over.

The first time you surrender to a particular feeling it may feel like you're drowning in the emotion. That is to be expected but the next time it won't be quite so overwhelming. And so on, until you hardly notice it. Each time you let go it feels like a weight has been lifted and you will look and feel lighter.

The same applies to thoughts or other events that trigger you such as when you see 'happy families'. Notice the thought and then allow the associated feelings to come and to go.

Sometimes it might feel as if nothing has changed; be patient with yourself. Maybe start by letting go of small things, then notice how much you are progressing and how it becomes easier with time.

There will be times when feeling everything is just not feasible or practical because of the rush of emotions or if you're in a public place. For example you don't want to break down completely in the supermarket. So be aware of these times and be compassionate with yourself. The most important thing is to take small steps.

A great way to start learning to let go is by using Emma's Let Go of The Body Exercise, which is at the end of the chapter. It is also an effective way to release tension and tightness in the body.

Marking The Ending

Rituals are important to us. They mark transitions and rites of passage. Throughout our lives we mark changes in our identity with ceremonies but there's no funeral for the loss of a dream. What all these ceremonies have in common is that they draw a line in the sand so that when you step over it, you are different. You'll read in the following stories how I and the storytellers felt after our ceremony (whatever it was), and then you can decide if a ceremony would help you.

My Story: A New Start in the Grand Canyon

The process of getting to know what emotions feel like, letting them go, and noticing that they pass has been transformational for me in many ways. It has also enabled me to reconnect with my body, which, as you'll read in the next chapter, has changed me fundamentally.

I spent years hiding my feelings and most importantly not showing them on the outside, so becoming more open has taken time. I started to learn in the safe place of my therapist's office as she encouraged me to feel and to let go. At first feeling and crying were really hard, and I was encouraged by how liberated and lighter I felt afterwards.

I'm learning through experience that I am in control of how much I let go. When I'm in my therapist's office or my personal yoga lesson, I tend to let emotions take their course, knowing that they will subside when they're ready. At other times or places, I decide, dependent on how I feel. On a yoga weekend, I was first triggered by a meditation. I really wanted to sit and cry but it was just before breakfast so I put the emotions aside, had breakfast and then went back into the meditation room to let go of what had come up. Later in the day we had a session of transformational breathwork, which triggered me big time.

After a while I decided, for today, this is enough, so I pulled back and allowed the wave to subside. I was proud of my awareness and self-care, both of which are also new for me.

The box that once held everything I didn't want to feel outside me has gone forever, and in its place I *feel* everything inside. Emotions no longer burst out of me, I can feel them surging in my chest and decide whether or not to allow them to rise up and out of my eyes. It's as though I now have a tap in my throat, which I can choose whether to open or not.

There is something special about allowing the soft roll of tears to flow and noticing how it connects me deeply to myself. And when it ebbs, embracing the feelings both of emptiness and stillness that follow.

My yoga teacher Emma observed that I almost look happy when I'm crying, and that is true because each time I let something go, I feel like I'm shedding another layer of the armour that prevents me from being my authentic self. I am often surprised, as I realise just how much I've changed since that day in Vegas, at the Brené Brown Rising Strong workshop.

I know that I still have more grief to let go of, and that's okay. I am now a lot more resilient so what used to take a wave to knock me over; now takes a tsunami. My focus is to continue exploring and letting go as opportunities arise.

This is also true in other areas of my life. Sometimes I can be like a dog with a bone, especially when I want someone else to change a behaviour that irritates me. That is, until I remember that I can't change someone else, and (as I wrote in Chapter Four), I am in control of my response. I then make a conscious effort to let go. Being completely honest, this is a challenge for me and can take a while, and many times I have to say 'let go, let go'.

Letting go has opened up so many more possibilities to me. Before I started to let go and open myself up to feeling, I was numb and stuck. As you'll read in Chapter Thirteen, letting go of grief and sadness has opened me up to feeling so much more happiness and joy.

I've also let go of expectation, especially of what I can and can't do, most of which has happened on the yoga mat. In terms of letting go, what I've learned, is that when I let go of what the asana, or pose should look like, or how far I *think* my body can bend or stretch; it surprises me, every time. When my mind relaxes my body follows and does things it's never done before. Afterward, I always feel energised and empowered to achieve even more.

And now to the Grand Canyon.

My ceremony happened by accident. For our 10th wedding anniversary, Roger and I took a river trip on the Colorado River through the Grand Canyon. Maybe you've seen the canyon from the top. Well, it's a completely different experience from the bottom. You spend two weeks travelling into the depths of the canyon and the earth and back out again. All who take the trip are changed by the experience, including me.

It was in the stillness and quiet of her depths (because the canyon is definitely a she) that I heard her voice assuring me that I could have a wonderful life without children. At that stage it was a whisper and it continued to be there quietly in my unconscious.

Seven years later I heard her call again so we booked another trip. There's a saying that you can never travel the same river twice and it's true. Sleeping on the ground was still hard and the water was still cold and exhilarating but I decided to challenge myself in new ways.

From the riverbank at the bottom of a canyon a mile deep, the only way is up. So one morning we got up at 4am, put on our head torches and started to climb. The aim was to get to the top of a 2,200ft peak in time to see the sunrise.

It was hot, dark, and dusty; one of those climbs where you think you're at the top and then there's another hill, and another. My thighs were screaming and I was really struggling. I stopped and told Roger that I'd had enough. He said: 'If you don't get to the top, you'll regret it for the rest of your life.' And he was right. I knew deep down that I would.

With a monumental effort I pushed myself to reach the top. Once I got there, I felt completely authentic, as though I'd finally emerged into the light after many years in the dark. I felt free and completely, 100% me for the first time in years. I'd been struggling for so long to work out who I am in the world, and in that moment, everything and anything seemed possible.

All of a sudden the voice that had been a whisper became louder and so many new possibilities opened up as I realised, *yes* I can do this; I can have a great life without children.

Standing at the top, something shifted and walking down I felt freer and more like myself than I had in many years.

It fascinates me that my 'ending' occurred on a peak called The Tabernacle, which is an ancient Hebrew word with various meanings including, *any place or house of worship*, a *portable sanctuary* and *the human body regarded as the temporary dwelling of the soul*, because my climb was like a pilgrimage, something I *had* to do. Was it important that I wouldn't have got there without Roger's encouragement? Probably. Because it is hard to do this alone.

Below is **Louise's** experience of 'marking the ending'.

My simple Christian faith has helped me. I often repeat the words of the Lord's prayer '...Thy will be done...' when I am stuck and can't fathom out why I am where I am. In 2012, I felt a service of thanksgiving would be a good way to recognise my thanks for the opportunity to create life, even though the IVF was ultimately unsuccessful, and to acknowledge the good times in our marriage.

Andrew agreed to join me for this, which pleased me. It would help us acknowledge many things that had been left unsaid. The service was just for the two of us. We could have invited others but this was not a celebration. It was an ending for us and it was important for me that it was a private ending without others shedding tears. With help from the priest we wrote a short service. We started with a reading from the Bible that we had chosen for our wedding service. I Corinthians 13, 'Love is patient and kind.... Love bears all things, believes all things, hopes all things, endures all things.... Love never ends.'

I loved the reading. Although the love we felt for each other on our wedding day had long since died as it was not strong enough to 'bear all things', hearing it again as we stood there together in front of the altar was comforting. In common with many faiths, lighting candles feature in many Christian services. We took turns to light candles to give thanks for our marriage, the doctors and nurses who had treated us, Andrew's children and my nieces and nephews, the love of our family and friends.

We also acknowledged the pain of our separation and for the last candle we committed to trust that God would go with us as we moved on with our lives. This was the most significant candle in my healing. I was about to take a big step in my life and move to Malawi to work.

The final prayers sent us out into the world in peace. I felt peace although we were no longer joined by love and I missed that, I knew the road ahead was bright and one I could face alone.

Here's a description of the stones ritual that **Jill Duffin** did to mark her ending.

Start with a basket of stones. They are symbols of whatever burdens we have picked up on our fertility paths.

Choose one that may symbolise the weight in your heart or stomach connected to your journey that you would like to release or leave behind. If you can, give it a name or symbol. Give yourself time to reflect and write or draw something on it.

Now chose another stone, which will symbolise where you would like to be in the future. On it write down or draw the positive qualities that have come out of your fertility experience. For me it was words like courage, wisdom, compassion. The idea is that these qualities may be trying to be born within us. Keep this stone and place it somewhere meaningful for you.

After the ceremony we took the stones outside and threw them into a pond. I chose to keep the positive quality stone and still have it today.

This ritual is taken from Meredith Wheeler's notes on holding a ceremony for fertility loss.

Karen Malone Wright went to a retreat for 'pregnancy loss'. Here are the key points and you can learn more on our video.

I went into it broken. I was in a bad, sad place. If I saw a visibly pregnant woman I could get weepy, whether it was in real life or on TV. One day I saw a visibly pregnant women drinking a beer and I walked right up to her and said 'are you crazy, you can't do that'. I was just broken. The time I realised I wasn't going to have kids, was the time I realised, you're an only child, if you don't have children, all of your families' history, all that they fought for to get to where you are, it dissipates so you'd better hurry up and do something wonderful to make your families' name.

Everyone's story was different; the women defined pregnancy loss in their own way. In the morning we each made a flag where each square represented something in your life that led you to be there that day. It was like a knitting group, women getting together talking about the things we don't usually talk about.

Everyone was told to bring an item that represented their lost baby. Many brought a toy. You hit a large gong and announced the baby's name. Every woman knew what that name would have been. Then you walked alone into an outdoor labyrinth. You left the item at the centre. It was a huge labyrinth so you truly were alone. When you walked out of the labyrinth, you had, in so many ways left that baby behind and said goodbye. Then you hit the gong again, and said your own name.

I don't know that I felt anything at that moment but when I got home, my husband took one look at me and said, 'I don't know what it did but it changed you. You look lighter.'

I think we all look to find acceptance with our reality and it was a physical manifestation of that acceptance. Every woman had a toy or blanket in their attic or basement taking up space in her life. All these years, waiting for this baby to appear. Just the physical-ness of going to get the item, touching it, crying over it, driving it out to this cottage and leaving it there. It was a tangible thing.

Each of our storytellers felt different after the ceremony. And they *were* all different, so we can see that the event in itself isn't as important as the spirit in which it's carried out.

Let's Talk About Resistance

Even after reading these stories you might be feeling some resistance. Let me reassure you that it is completely natural. You've had this dream for a long time, and it's natural that you are reluctant to let it go. It's also useful to recognise how you think you are benefitting from staying stuck and what you believe the advantages are.

So ponder these questions for a few moments, as they'll help you to get to the root of this resistance. Then write down your answers.

a. What will happen if I let go of the dream?

b. What won't happen if I let go of the dream?

c. What will happen if I don't let go of the dream? (If I don't let go, I will...)

d. What won't happen if I don't let go of the dream? (If I don't let go, I won't...)

These aren't easy questions and your answers will be revealing. It will be worth taking the time to think deeply about them and exploring them in your writing practice. Ask yourself, 'When is enough, enough?' How much longer are you willing to be miserable?

Journaling Questions

- What are the key things you've learned from this chapter?

- Which areas would be helpful for you to explore? Examine these as you write in your journal.

  Ask yourself the questions I posed earlier in the chapter:

- What am I willing to give up, in order to have a new life? What's stopping me from achieving my greatest potential?

- If you still have resistance, go back to the visualisation you did at the end of Act One. Do you really want your life to stay the same as it is now? That is what will happen if you don't start letting go.

- Practice letting go of feelings as they come up. Notice how much easier it becomes with time. When something comes up, and you're not sure whether you want to let it go, or not, ask yourself 'if I hang on to this, will it lead to more pain and sadness?' If you find it hard, repeating 'let it go, let it go' either out loud or in your head as you work through it, will help it to flow quicker.

- Go around your house and gather up everything that's in your museum to grief.

- What expectations do you have about what's possible for you and your life?

Here's **Emma Peel's Let Go of the Body Exercise**, which I mentioned earlier in the chapter. It is a great way to start learning to let go (you can listen to us discuss it on the video).

I lay on my back, arms away from the body, space between the heels, hands shoulders and ears. I visualise every aspect of my body letting go.

I start with the right thumb, and I'll go through the fingers, the palm of the hand, the back of the hand, wrist, and I'll travel up the arm the shoulder, back of the shoulder, front of the shoulder. I'll work up the left arm, and I'll work all the way down the body and each toe.

I'll imagine each individual part of my body letting go so I can really feel the concept of letting go.

I can also feel where there was holding in my body. For example, I was holding tension in my jaw.

It's a really weird concept to imagine letting go of your right ear, but as you let go of the noise and movement outside and really bring that awareness into your body, you can understand letting go from a physical perspective. This practice allows you to feel with your inner self.

Ceremony.

- Consider whether a ceremony would help you and what it might be. Could any of those used by the storytellers work for you, or would you prefer something different? Other options could be:

  - Writing down all your hopes and dreams on a sheet of paper, then burning it, burying it, or throwing it in a river or the sea.

  - Creating a special time to spend with your partner, somewhere different.

  - Planting a tree or a rose bush in a place you can visit.

- If you have a toy or clothes you bought for your child, ask yourself what would be the best thing to do with them? Maybe you could take them to a children's hospital, hospice, or charity, or maybe what would work best is destroying them.

- The same applies to other memorabilia you've held on to. Before you destroy any journals or diaries, you might consider writing your story so read the chapter on writing first.

- Now go and do it, then notice how different you feel.

Chapter Eight
What's That Below Your Head?
Reconnecting With Your Body

I believe your body knows a lot more than your mind about the life you're supposed to live.

Martha Beck, from
Finding Your Own North Star

When recently talking to a good friend, she was surprised when I mentioned I was writing a chapter about connecting to your body. 'I've never really thought about it', she said.

Until I started working with a therapist, I hadn't thought about my body in that way either; it was the thing that carried my head around. As it emerged as an important theme in a number of stories, I thought I should investigate it and since I've been exploring and connecting to it, I can say that I have never felt more alive both physically and emotionally. As you'll read, my body has also played an important role in debunking many limiting beliefs (such as how far I can stretch in yoga), therefore enabling my mind to follow.

Like in all the other chapters, in this one I invite you to read with an attitude of curiosity and be open to the possibility that an increased connection to your body might make a difference to you in the same way it has to me and the other ladies whose stories I share. Your body is going to be with you all your life, so it makes sense to get to know it and take care of it, right?

Let's start with some basics.

What I Know About My Body

I know these things about my body:

- It will be with me all my life and I'd like that to be a long time, so it makes sense to look after it.

- I put it through some pretty challenging things and it let me down big time.

- There is a strong mind/body link.

- Stress and trauma are stored in it.

Let's explore these last two ideas a bit more.

The mind/body link.

I've written about this already in the chapter on grief, where I encouraged you to start realising how different emotions feel in your body. Hopefully by now you're starting to notice how strong this link is.

Research has shown that your brain communicates through the body via neurotransmitters which send impulses along your nerves. In *The Complete Guide to Yin Yoga: The Philosophy and Practice of Yin Yoga*, Bernie Clark discusses how this connection between heart, mind, and body works. Clark explains that your heart is the seat of emotions, mind is the seat of thoughts and body is your physical home. When one is stimulated, the others react. An emotion arises in your heart, and this stimulates your physical body; you secrete hormones (adrenaline) and get ready to fight, for flight, or to freeze. Your heart rate rises and you're ready for action. At the same time this creates thoughts in your mind and you start making up a story about what's happening, and who is good and who is bad.

Can you see that it's a cycle? Emotions stimulate the physical body, the physical body stimulates the mind, and the mind stimulates emotions. Brené Brown found in her research that when something happens, your emotions kick in first, thinking and behaviour take much longer to react. As I wrote in the grief chapter, it's not possible to stop strong emotions from arising, but it is possible to change your thoughts and not to suffer because of them.

If you're not yet convinced, think of a time when you got anxious or stressed (maybe a three out of ten). Go back to that moment and relive it, see what you saw, hear what you heard, and now feel what you felt. Notice what's happening in your body when you think back to that time. For example, when I get stressed or anxious I want to shrink and I feel like I'm rooted to the spot, whilst at the same time my mind is telling me to run. Most often I'll shrink into myself, and now that I've noticed this I've given myself permission to walk away if that's more appropriate.

Shake that off and now do the same with a time when you felt joyful and happy. Notice how very different your body feels now. Mine feels a lot more expansive and lighter when I re-live a happy experience. What about yours?

In her talk *Refuge in the Wilderness,* Tara Brach describes connecting to our body as 'coming back to our senses' and I like this way of describing what we're doing here.

Your body stores stress and trauma.

There's plenty of research showing that everything which happens to you leaves physiological imprints on your body, especially when you experience situations that cause your fight, flight, or freeze response to be triggered. Your body remembers it all.

I've read two books that explore this in more detail: *Waking The Tiger: Healing Trauma* by Peter Levine and *The Body Keeps The Score: Mind, Brain and Body in the Transformation of Trauma* by Bessel Van Der Kolk. From my reading, I understand the human brain has three integral systems, the reptilian brain (instinctual), the mammalian or limbic brain (emotional), and the human brain or neo-cortex (rational). When faced with a threat your instinctual and emotional brains take charge. That makes sense, doesn't it?

The authors have also proved that trauma and stress are stored in the body. Have you ever watched a wildlife documentary where a deer escaped being chased by a cheetah? As a last ditch strategy it becomes frozen, then it escapes the chase and once it's free it shakes all over. The shaking releases the energy that was trapped by the trauma of the chase. This doesn't always happen with us. Sometimes we go into that frozen state and the energy stays there, trapped.

My understanding is that we've all experienced some sort of trauma where the energy of the trauma has remained in our body. This makes sense to me; the last time I got on a bicycle I fell off, and just thinking about getting back on makes my whole body tense up as it remembers the stress and anxiety I felt.

Does that make sense? Are there times when your body remembers similar stressful incidents? Of course, the reverse will also be true. It will also remember being joyful and loved.

It follows that healing the body will also heal the mind. That's certainly been my experience.

Here are two examples:

> **Emily Jacob**: I think there are lots of different experiences that can be traumatic. Anything that really disconnects us and has that real physical separation between body, mind, or soul creates a huge, almost Grand Canyon-like chasm between those different parts of you. Anything that does that has a traumatic impact on us that we then need to work through.
>
> **Rosalind Bubb**: I haven't ever *felt* as if I've had an issue with my body, in connection to being childless. Every time I did EFT 'tapping', I said the words 'I deeply and completely love and accept myself' (because it's part of the process to say this, or some alternative, positive phrase.) And this is the reason, I believe, that I've never felt as if my body has let me down.

As a result of the EFT, I've loved it and accepted it, and I haven't blamed it, or myself, for the fact that I haven't been able to have children. (And I'm very grateful for that.) That doesn't mean that there weren't still things going on that needed to be addressed, however!

For a number of years, I had a very bad back. I went to see a specialist Pilates teacher, who concluded that my twelve miscarriages had resulted in my pelvic floor muscles being traumatised. It was if the muscles had been pulled up very, very tightly for years, trying to hold my babies in my womb. (Indeed, all of my miscarriages had been 'missed': it always took a very long time for my body to finally let the babies go.)

The Pilates specialist gave me some exercises to try to get these traumatised muscles to relax. Ordinarily, she would have expected this to take months, but I used TAT (Tapas Acupressure Technique) to release the trauma from my body (which only took twenty minutes) and consequently my pelvic floor muscles *did* relax and let go, all very suddenly. This caused a gigantic crisis, because all the other muscles which 'should' have been doing the work (instead of the pelvic floor ones) weren't ready to take over. I had to re-learn which muscles in my pelvis and my back were supposed to be taking the strain, which took a very long time.

About a year and a half later, she said that all the muscles *below* my pelvis were working fine, and all the ones *above* it were also as they should be. But she said that it was as if there was a 'block' in the middle, and the two areas of my body weren't talking to each other.

She brought one of her anatomy books and showed me line drawings of the pelvis, and how the muscles support the uterus, ovaries, and fallopian tubes. What I discovered was that I couldn't even bring myself to *say* the words 'womb', 'uterus' or 'ovaries' without feeling as if I was going to cry.

You might have heard of a phenomenon call 'dissociation'. This is when someone experiences something really traumatic and terrifying being done to their body, and it can feel as if they're rising up out of themselves and are up somewhere near the ceiling, looking down at what's happening to them below.

The reason for this is that if you *stayed* in your body while you were experiencing that level of overwhelming stress and terror, it would be more than your system could physically take. And so we dissociate ourselves from what's happening, to keep ourselves safe.

I realised that it felt as if all the internal organs from my pelvis had dissociated: when I thought about them, it felt as if they were all about two metres to the right of my body. And they felt black, as if they'd shut down and gone into a state of suspension. I think they'd been traumatised when I lost so much blood during the operation after my 14-week miscarriage.

Over the course of three months we healed all my miscarriage traumas, using TAT. It felt as if the organs moved back into my body, and they became the right colour again, and they returned to active life and felt loved, safe, connected, and peaceful. And my back is now doing extremely well. All the connections are flowing again, without any blocks, just as it should be.

I find all of this really startling! I'd had no idea that this was going on: it had never occurred to me. I suspect that many women may have gone through this kind of trauma. Fertility treatment and miscarriages can be really distressing, embarrassing, and painful, and I think there can be all sorts of times and situations when parts of our bodies can become dissociated, contracted, or traumatised.

The key is to ask the question: how does my body feel? What's my relationship with it? What does it need, and what can I do to help it? And try different methods, until you find what suits you.

The healing tools I used, EFT 'tapping' and TAT, are both called 'energy techniques'. You can use them to change your feelings and your emotions, and they can help you to feel calmer and happier. In addition to this, they affect the energy systems and connections throughout our minds and bodies. When we use these therapeutic self-help tools, we're not just talking or thinking about it. We're actually changing the ways our bodies are functioning. Traumas, grief and events that have been 'stuck' in our body can be released and healed, and no longer cause us any problems.

Rosalind's experience is extreme and, having researched I agree that in a traumatic event, for protection and survival the brain can separate from the body – or dissociate. You can also dissociate in daily life when you do something and can't remember having done it. Perhaps you felt 'spaced out'. If you're depressed, you may also dissociate from the world and from yourself. If you're experiencing this, please seek professional help.

In the same way, unprocessed grief and other emotions also become trapped in your body. They can stay there for as long as it takes you to summon up the courage to express them or until (as in my case) they keep leaking out. To become whole, this trapped energy must be released.

My Story: I Am My Body. No, Now I Am My Body. No, Now Really...

I never really thought about my body. It was just the thing that carried me around. I fuelled it, and that was it. It let me down though, a number of times. Maybe I didn't think this consciously but I acted as if it was the case. I ate unhealthily and didn't really exercise. I was ambivalent about it.

Maybe more than that, I was ashamed of it. I mean it couldn't hang on to an embryo, not once but six times. In my mind I disliked it because it couldn't do the thing that *every other woman in the world* can do. Of course, I knew logically that it wasn't 'every other' woman but in the early days that was certainly how I felt.

Then two things happened. I have already told you that the Rising Strong workshop in Vegas was the first time I made the connection between what was going on in my mind and what was happening in my body, as I realised that feelings are called feelings because you actually *feel* them in your body. This was *massive* for me, as if a whole new world was opening up.

Then, out of the blue my therapist asked me how I felt about my body. Saying out loud that I felt disconnected from it started what I hope will be a long and beautiful friendship with it.

I started by being kind, asking, 'what would I do if I loved my body and cared about it?' and acting accordingly. Starting to respect and be grateful for it. I also noticed the ways I thought about it and specifically nourished it with words and actions. It was about this time that I read the books I mentioned above, *Waking The Tiger* by Peter Levine and *The Body Keeps The Score* by Bessel Van Der Kolk, so I was open to the possibility that connecting to my body could make a difference.

Adventuring on to the yoga mat.

My therapist suggested that I do Jon Kabat-Zinn's MBSR programme, which led me to yoga. I found a local studio and off I went in my tracksuit bottoms and baggy T-shirt (there was no way I was wearing leggings you understand, not with my thighs) expecting that *everyone else* there would be in their 20s and as thin as a stick. But did that matter? No, it didn't. I tried a number of different classes and found that I loved Yin most of all. Holding the asanas for three to five minutes is hard and in those minutes I started to listen to my body and be with it.

I am my body.

Another piece of the jigsaw was having sessions of Cranio Sacral Therapy (CST). Helen Rebello suggested it would help my body recover from the shock of a sprained ankle and it did a lot more than that.

Research tells me that CST is a gentle way of working with the body using light touch. It works with the whole person and changes may occur in body, mind and spirit. The therapist uses her hands to listen to you in much the same way that other kinds of therapists might listen to your words. Your body responds to this by beginning to listen to itself, and to balance, restore and heal itself.

My experience is that you lie on a couch (fully clothed), and then the therapist touches various parts of your body and wonderful things happen. Some of my experiences have included feeling relaxed, peaceful, calm, definitely more balanced, and most importantly for me, knowing that I was making big steps towards really connecting with my body. One week I said something I would never have dreamed of saying before: '*I am my body*'.

No, *now* I am my body; discovering Yin Yoga.

The final piece of this jigsaw was deciding that, as I love Yin Yoga most of all, private lessons would be useful. That was when I discovered many things about myself and my body. Many times in my life I've asked for help with one thing and my unconscious knew that I needed something different. I thought I wanted to know how to do the asanas so I asked Emma Peel my yoga teacher to teach me. Of course she did this, but both she and my unconscious knew that what I really wanted was to deepen my mind/body connection, to learn about my feelings, to release those trapped emotions, to release many limiting beliefs and, almost as a side effect, to become more supple and bendy than I've ever been in my life.

Coming home to the breath.

Breath is fundamental in both yoga and meditation and becoming conscious of my breath has helped me so much. I notice how my breath speeds up and gets shallower when I get tense, and equally how slow breathing quietens my mind, puts it into a relaxed internal state, and sends a message to my body that it is safe and calm. This is a great reset, and when I want to slow down, I breathe in and out to a count of four, five, or six, which immediately slows me down and puts me back into my body.

I can feel my breath in different parts of my body, too. I can breathe into my belly, chest, and ribs and I can feel it as it energises my whole body.

Noticing my breath also puts me in the present, because you can only breathe in the present. In Act One I wrote about the space between stimulus and response; I use my breath to expand that space, to take a step back and be more conscious of my response.

I discussed this space and using breath as an anchor with **Emma Peel**, and here's a summary of our discussion. At the end of this chapter Emma also suggests a simple breathing exercise.

> Breath is an anchor. It creates this sense of stability, and a breath awareness practice delivers you into the present moment and a present moment that is awake. It's an active engagement; it delivers you from the past and stops you projecting into the future. It delivers you right here.

There is a simplicity of *now*; so if you're walking, feel the cool air on your face, reminding yourself of the joy of living and being alive.

It's so simple.

It's a practice you can feel with the whole body and with the mind. You can learn how to softly control the breath, to deepen it and feel it move through your whole body. It brings the mind from up here in the head and drops it down into the body where you can feel.

Viktor E. Frankl said that 'between stimulus and response there is a space...'; by using that space you will become more conscious of your response. By doing this you have the space to take a step back, take a breath and see the totality rather than one aspect. That's the breath practice for us to see the totality of something, the wholeness rather than just the one aspect we were focusing on. It's also a reminder of letting go, and what it feels like to let things drop off in order to let in something new.

The important thing is we're not looking to make or create anything. It's all here. We're just working with what we have.

With a breath practice we become aware of when the breath stops or is interrupted. We tend to hold a lot of emotions in the chest, and when we're stressed the breath is shallow so breathing into the belly is really helpful. We notice the complete flow in and out, and notice how energy slowly calms and moves in the body.

It's easy for energy to fly up and be in your thinking mind; breathing into your belly brings you back to your centre of action and power, and into the body.

I think the most important thing is we want to experience things as they are. So be with the breath as it is.

If we observe the breath as it is, simply by breathing in and breathing out, over and over, we become aware of it. If the breath is short, the breath is short and if the breath is long, the breath is long. It's our first invitation to being with things exactly as they are. You give yourself the space to observe it, to know that you have the tools to control both the breath and your response.

In our Yin practice we're learning to discern. Is it something painful? And if it is, how should you adjust yourself or should you shift your perspective? The challenge is to sit in that essence of discomfort and to find peace there. It is to be the space and to find the centre which is grounded and anchored in the present moment.

I agree with Emma completely. Noticing my breath, and, when it would be helpful, controlling it, has changed so much for me.

Becoming a Yin Yogi.

I love the meditations of Tara Brach and she often refers to the body as a *'field of sensations'*. At first, I couldn't get this at all. Of course, I can feel my feet on the floor, but anything inside? No. Now that I've been practicing Yin for almost two years, I really understand what she means. As I type this, yes of course I can feel where different parts of my body are touching the floor, chair, and laptop. And more than this I can feel from the inside out, there's tingling in my arms, down my back and all through my legs. My body really does feel like the field of sensations Tara mentions. I can feel this all the time now, and it is absolutely wonderful.

I know now that this tingling is energy moving; sometimes it's the energy that needs to move for me to express and heal my grief. When this energy (whatever it may be, sometimes it's joy, pain, anger) rises to the surface and I let it flow I ask myself, 'when have I felt this before', 'what's my mind telling me that's different from my body', and 'what does this mean?' In this way I've learned to recognise how different emotions feel. Sometimes I realise what thought or feeling has triggered them, other times I don't. And it's okay. The main thing is to let them flow. In the safe space of Emma's Yoga Den, I've released so much.

I am now more attentive, still, and patient. As someone who finds sitting still under any circumstance to be a *real* challenge and has never been called patient in her life, you'll understand how much I'm changing. I stretch my body to the edge of where it can go, I breathe to that edge and into the discomfort, and ask myself over and over, 'can I be with this?' Almost always the answer is 'yes' and after a while I notice that the discomfort has lessened and I can push beyond my previous boundary. Sometimes this is a small movement, and other times it is a massive stretch.

When I'm being challenged, my breath shortens and my perspective narrows. I recall one time my breath was shallow and I was hanging onto the blanket as if my life depended on it. Once Emma pointed it out, I relaxed my grip, took a few conscious and slow breaths and felt a lot calmer.

I realise how much I notice when I'm paying attention. For example, in a standing meditation, moving my weight from over my heels to my toes changes everything (discovering this made me cry).

I've become aware of the subtle and fascinating way that everything in my body is connected. I ask myself questions like, 'what's my left hip doing now and the right; how are they different? If I make this adjustment, what changes? Where can I relax where I didn't realise I was tense?' As I get to know its subtleties, I notice that it reacts in specific ways, and I ask whether this is helping me or putting up a barrier.

I am using my body much more, and I love how it feels when I challenge it. Our last holiday included a six-day sea kayaking trip that was very physically challenging for me and a long way outside my comfort zone. On day three I was spent emotionally and physically, and once I'd rested, I had the same wonderful feeling of achievement and strength that I get on the yoga mat.

After a while I understood what Tara was saying and I realised that my body is always talking. It has always been talking and it's only by being quiet and still that I can hear it.

No, now I really am my body, letting it lead the way.

After practicing Yin for a year, my body started to lead my mind. Let's go back to the story I told in Act One about how changing the story I was telling myself from one of impossibility to possibility, opened my body up to achievement.

The first time I achieved Saddle, as I was lying there, stretched out, open and vulnerable, the wonderful Emma told me more about it and what she said underlined exactly why it's important to me. It turns out that the meaning of Saddle is Hero, and as you know a Hero (or Heroine) goes through challenges, which she tries to solve easily, and in the end the only way she can get to where she wants to be is by changing herself.

That is my story in writing this book. It is yours, too.

Each time I move into Saddle, I'm aware that I am exposed, laying my heart and vulnerability bare for all to see. I can feel the power and strength in my body, as I connect very deeply with me. Staying there takes everything I've learned, and all the courage, strength, and trust I can muster. It's teaching me that connecting to my heart connects me to my deepest meaning and purpose; it encourages me to be fearless and to realise my potential. It is connecting me to the strength within my core. In Indian Chakras this is Manipura, the centre of personal power and warrior energy. It's the centre of self-esteem, confidence, taking responsibility for one's life, making decisions, and self-assurance.

It is my seat. It is telling the story of me.

A story of strength, power, and heart connection.

I've also learned how close my mind/body connection is and how it changes. Sometimes I can stay in Saddle for many minutes, laughing and chatting with Emma, while other times it is difficult. When I confirmed the publication date for this book, I was rocked emotionally as I realised that I would soon be holding it and it would be a physical reality. After a few days I thought I was back to (a new) normal, but my body would not bend itself into Saddle, not even with a bolster. In the past I would have beaten myself up and pushed my body beyond where it wanted to go; not this time. Now that I'm listening to my body, I am gentle and kind and, a couple of weeks later, when my mind and body were ready, there I was comfortably back in Saddle.

I've also learned to let go of my limitations and expectations on the mat. There have been other times when I've told myself that I can't do something (yes, I know I'm a slow learner), and when I let this go, I achieve much more. Saying 'I can't do that' is an invitation to Emma, and before I know what's happened I am upside down or sitting in Half Lotus position.

What my body can do and how far it can stretch has astounded me many times. I am more bendy and supple than I have ever been in my life. Each time my body does something unexpected; another belief I had about my limitations is shattered. Each week it shows me that it can do more and more, and where my body goes, my mind follows.

If my body is telling a story of determination, strength, power, and achievement, why shouldn't my mind?

If I can do these physical things, why can't I do other things?

If the limitations I had about my body no longer apply, what about those other beliefs I had about what I can or can't achieve?

When I started this work, I regarded my body as the thing that carried my head around. Now? Well I'm proud of it, amazed at what it can do, and I respect and nurture it. I'm not yet ready to say that I love it, but I'm almost there. I also know that it has things to say, and I'm listening.

You can see an image of me in Saddle with the resources.

How I've changed.

Since doing this work many friends have said that I look different, especially lighter and I'm certainly more content, confident, grounded, and comfortable in my own skin. I'm also more sensitive to sounds, tastes and colours and I feel much more alive. Mostly, I feel a deep inner peace and calm.

I realise my unconscious mind wanted me to connect to my body. By doing so I've peeled off many layers that were hiding the real me so I could become that beautiful butterfly that was hiding inside.

If you're still not convinced, here are some more experiences.

Helen Rebello

For me connecting to my body was key because as far as I was concerned it had let me down in many ways. I had a lot of reasons to be very cross with my body, but you can't run away from it. It's the house you live in. You start to recognise that when you view it negatively or you're not really connecting with it and have less of a foundation in which to live your life, you're disconnected from the neck down and not living as intentionally as you should.

The more you dislike or hate your body the more you start to break yourself physically. For me it was eating the wrong stuff, then physical symptoms. I was achy and stiff, had low energy levels and would often crash.

One of the simplest of things with yoga was feeling into your feet, and the ability of them to walk you around.

Jessica Hepburn

I'm still in the process of really trying to understand my body. I had unexplained infertility and feel that it has failed and not done what it's supposed to do, and that's hard to live with every day.

My instinct is that my body was too strong, too masculine and that it was fighting. I'm still in that dialogue with the power of the body and it's interesting that I've gone on to do these very masculine challenges.

These challenges – climbing mountains and swimming seas – have been about reconnecting with nature and understanding that we can't control it. You can only climb a mountain if it decides to let you. And your body will only let you conceive a baby if it decides to do so.

These challenges are about a celebration of the thing that I felt my body was, which was strong and prevented me from having a child. That's my instinct. They are also about accepting my vulnerability in nature. That's become a very big theme of who I am and what I'm writing about now.

And more from **Emily Jacob**

I'd got a handle on the psychological symptoms of trauma, and I was no longer depressed or subject to panic attacks because of the rape. I'd worked a lot on my thought processes and my brain, and I understood the place I wanted to have in the world. I had forgiven the world a little bit. But I still felt very fragile and broken.

It was a real lightbulb moment when I realised I was very much disconnected and dissociated from my body. It was just this vehicle that I lugged around in life rather than it being part of *me*.

I realised that during trauma, my body had experienced it and my mind had checked out and left it to it. I had detached and built up this habit of total dissociation and detachment from it.

My body needed to forgive my brain as well as my brain forgive my body for what happened. My body had let me down throughout my entire adult life because it had never behaved the way it was supposed to.

It's been a journey of self-awareness around that, acknowledging that this package I'm in is part of me and not just a package. Self-compassion must happen both ways; my body needs to forgive too. This realisation was like: oh my God I am one whole being. It's not just the brain that functions.

I took baby steps to self-compassion and self-love, slowly experiencing what that felt like. It started with deciding that I was worth having a bath with bubbles. With deciding that actually I could moisturise my legs with body cream; to recognise that they belonged to me and they deserved to be smooth. Rather than slapping it on, I started to create a ritual, almost a sensual way of applying cream to my body. To show my body that it was being loved and cherished and treasured. I also like to let loose and dance in my kitchen.

I'm doing small things mindfully; getting my body and me together is still a process. I use the term bodyful because it is our compass. It has all the answers.

When we're starting to feel emotions, we can be mindful of those emotions; and we can feel them in our body first. We can ask ourselves, why am I tensing? What is it that's making me tense right now? Is it reminding me of something that was dangerous in the past? What is this tension, and where am I feeling it? Is the tension I feel when I feel it in my fingers different from the tension I feel in my legs. The body is talking to us all the time and mostly we ignore it.

> I am really trying to listen to what my body is telling me on a minute-by-minute basis.
>
> This will be a lifelong practice. It helps me to realise when I'm tired and I need to replenish, and to know when I'm starting to get triggered or stressed about things before I've even got there. This means that I can do something about it.
>
> It has made me a much calmer person who can take more in my stride and appreciate all the work I've done on my ego, my conscious self, in terms of being that calm person. It's like just leaps and miles better, now that I've started to listen to my body.

Are you convinced yet?

Think of your body as your house, and the house you'll have for the rest of your life. Do you want to inhabit it, or *live* in it? *Living* and feeling alive is what I want and connecting to my body has made this happen more than anything else I've done.

Journaling Questions

- What are the key things you've learned from this chapter? Which areas would be helpful for you to explore? Examine these as you write in your journal.

Here's a selection of ways to take you out of your head and into your body.

- Notice how you talk to your body. What do you say to it? Are you kind? If not, how could you be kind, and how could you take care of it and nourish it?

- Start to wake up your body. Notice your feet on the floor, and be completely aware of them. If you're sitting, really feel the chair holding you. Do that several times a day. Then expand this to different areas of your body. When you're in bed, feel the sensation of the sheets as they touch your skin, and the bed holds you up.

- Stand barefoot on a flat surface, and rest on the earth. Be still, find your centre of gravity and notice how the arches of your feet are lifted off the ground. Spread your toes and notice that your weight is spread across all of them. Be aware of the muscles in your calves and thighs. Relax your knees. Make a small movement so that your weight shifts to your heels, how different does that feel? Can you feel the difference in your legs? Now bring your weight forward over your toes and see how different this feels.

- Next time you're in the shower or bath, consciously and slowly soap each part of your body, leisurely and gently, really feeling the sensations on your skin.

- What else can you do to connect to it? Go for a walk outside, swim, dance, sing maybe? Or take a walk. Being surrounded by elements outside connects you to what's inside you. Walk barefoot on the grass. Make a list of small things you can do to make that connection. And do them.

- How can you use your body more? Ask yourself, how could I stretch my body and do something outside my comfort zone, something I've never done before?

- I found Cranio Sacral Therapy to be really helpful and Rosalind used EFT and TAT. These are energy therapies.

You could perhaps investigate one of these or others such as Tai Chi, Shiatsu, Reflexology, Acupuncture, massage or others.

- Bessel Van Der Kolk recommends yoga to connect patients with their body. It has certainly helped me and Helen Rebello.

- Meditation can also be helpful in many ways. August and I started with Jon Kabatt Zinn's MBSR Programme. I also love Tara Brach's free meditations available on her website.

- And here's **Emma Peel's** suggestion to connect with your breath.

Sit or lay with one hand on your belly and one on your heart or chest.

Take three breaths drawing all the way down from the nostril, down and into the belly.

Feel the belly balloon into the palm so you're connecting to the physicality.

Let the breath leave.

Take three breaths like this and really connect with it. Feel the diaphragm drawing down, the belly expand and that fullness. Then arriving into emptiness as it leaves. Fullness and emptiness all in the breath.

On the next breath in, take it down into the belly and let it move up into the ribs. Feel the ribs expand and the sides of the body stretch out.

Exhale from the ribs and then the belly.

Take three breaths like this.

Now draw the breath down into the belly, up into the ribs, and then all the way up into the chest. Feel that full complete breath; a three-part breath

Then exhale from the top, chest, ribs, and belly.

Connect to the concentration and control as you breathe into the belly, ribs, and chest, and exhale from the chest ribs and belly, controlling the descent.

Feel that shift in the space you can create. You're not looking to do anything. Rather, you're looking to feel it. It's about going from empty to fullness, your own empty to fullness. You see growth and you see decline, as you remind yourself that is the nature of all things.

- Here's a useful mantra that **August** uses to catch herself when she's getting dragged into negative thinking or stressful thought cycles and needs to calm down.

Engage (telling myself to become aware of what I am thinking rather than just letting it happen and escalating unchecked),

Exhale (to connect with my breath and also to let out some of the negative build up I have just noticed),

Elevate (to try and step above the chaotic thought cycle, to watch it happening but not get dragged into its vortex, and in turn elevate my thoughts to a more positive place),

Enlighten (again two-fold in meaning, to enable me to literally lighten my mental load and also use this elevated and engaged state to connect with my inner voice/wisdom).

Chapter Nine
I Love And Accept Myself Completely As I Am

I am loved,
I love,
I love and accept myself completely as I am.

What happened in your mind and body when you read those words? Did you read them quickly, thinking *they don't apply to me?*

I've heard them before of course, and most recently in my private yoga lesson. When it came to the final sentence, I had a visceral reaction especially to the phrase 'love and accept myself'. I thought, *No.*

That's what this chapter is about, self-acceptance.

What is Self-Acceptance?

It's *when you accept yourself warts and all, despite your flaws, failures, and limitations. You forgive yourself and you let go of self-judgement. Instead of comparing yourself to others, you know you're enough just as you are. You stop worrying what others think so you relax and allow the inner, authentic, real you to be seen.*

There's a lot in that paragraph, and when I started writing I had mixed feelings about self-acceptance. On one hand it sounded really great and something I wanted, and on the other it seemed so completely unattainable that I didn't even want to try.

Read the paragraph again, slowly this time. Which words or phrases jump out at you?

I really connect with the final sentence, I'm pretty good at being the authentic me. In fact, it's the only way I know how to be, and I constantly surprise myself by how much I allow the inner me to be seen. Self-judgement though, that's another thing altogether. I'm great at beating myself up, and as for comparison, let's not even go there.

Let's dive straight in with words from **Cali Bird** as she describes her understanding of what self-acceptance is and how to do it.

Self-acceptance is one of those simple yet profoundly difficult concepts. It means to accept yourself as you are, warts and all. The trouble is, we don't want to do that. Very often we don't want to accept our wonderfulness and we want to fix our flaws.

Self-acceptance is about being comfortable with our dark side, or shadow self. It means that we have to accept that we might have weird attitudes about money, or that there are aspects of our lives we are embarrassed about.

I heard the term self-acceptance many times in my single journey, usually when I was sitting crying and lamenting over my fate to someone who was wiser than me. The first time I heard it I didn't get it. I thought, *Well I'm fine. I haven't had to deal with anything heavy like abuse or rape in my life so of course I accept myself. I'm fine.*

I kept hearing about it and it kept annoying me because I didn't get it. Some years later I decided to have therapy because I was starting to suffer from depression and the cracks in my fabulous exterior were showing. By this time, I knew that something else was going on under the surface of my life that was causing me unhappiness, so I was more open to self-acceptance. But then the question became how do you do self-acceptance?

I think it is a gentle kind process that accumulates over time. I needed to be told that everyone has a darker, less pleasant side that we do our best to hide from. Because everyone has this it helped me to know that I wasn't weird and I didn't have to be embarrassed about the aspects of me that I didn't like.

I think that gradually during this time I stopped putting on an act.

I was also following a personal development path. Louise Hay talks a lot about accepting our story and treating ourselves with kindness as though we were a little child. We wouldn't be hard on the child; we would love it. It gradually came down to, yes this is okay. There are good parts of me and bad parts, but they are all me.

What did we learn from Cali? To me the key points are:

- To accept yourself with all your wonderfulness and foibles.
- That it takes time.
- Being kind to yourself is key.

My Story: A Work In Progress

I've called this a 'work in progress', because it feels very much like that and I think that's the case for most of us. Going back a few years I would have said that self-acceptance, self-forgiveness, self-respect, and self-love were in a group of *things I'm not sure about*, which probably (well almost certainly) meant that they were areas I needed to work on. Well, I've done that.

Accepting my foibles.

Tara Brach, in her work on Radical Self-Acceptance says that there are two components to self-acceptance; they are mindfulness and love. She talks about needing to relate to the parts of ourselves that we've kept hidden and then to keep embracing those parts. I've already written about the importance of being more open about being childless but it's more than that. As Cali says, it's about truly accepting all those things that we don't like about ourselves.

What does that mean in practice? There are aspects of myself and my character that I'm not happy about, so taking what Tara says, I need to love and embrace them. There's a balance with wanting to change, too. How can I accept those things and still want to change them?

Let's go back to **Cali** for some 'how-to'.

How do you do self-acceptance? By being open to it. By knowing that you don't have to be perfect. By knowing that you are good enough just as you are. By knowing that you don't need fixing. By knowing that the way you are is complete for you and for the people around you. By having patience, with yourself and the process. By seeking help – for me it was a mixture of my Buddhist practice, therapy and personal development books and seminars. By living every day and finding the positives and the joy in your current circumstances. By knowing that no one else can make you happy, you have to find that happiness within yourself.

I journaled a lot, I wrote and I worked through the exercises in Julia Cameron's *The Artist's Way: A Course in Discovering and Recovering Your Creative Self*. On the page, it was important to be truly honest and open about how I was feeling, and to get everything out of my head and on the page. I was also doing my Buddhist chanting every day. You could also meditate or do something meditative like walking, running, or swimming regularly.

You have to self-nurture. You are on a tough enough journey so do little things for fun. For example, sit quietly with a coffee and read something enjoyable. Do activities that fill up your well. All of these little things accumulate over time. Gradually, you'll become more open to the concept that you are okay just as you are.

Ask yourself how can I be kind to myself? What's the kindest option? You are vulnerable on this journey, and it's okay that sometimes you'll be an emotional mess, very angry or in deep despair.

For me it was a gradual process over time, a multi-pronged journey where I learned more about the concept of self-acceptance as well as what made up the parts of myself. I'm much more grounded than I was. I don't have to be different because I'm with other people and I am comfortable in my own skin. I'm much more, *this is me, take it or leave it.*

I've talked through some of my 'foibles' with my therapist and I'm also learning to work with them in different ways. For example, Mum always said I was stubborn, and yes, it's true that I know what I want and don't like changing my mind once

I'm set on something. Taking what Cali says, I've accepted this *and* I'm learning to work with it in different ways. One way is to reframe it and call myself determined, which I like a lot better. Another is to be kind and gentle, to ask myself why do I find it hard to change my mind, what stops me, and what would happen if I was open to other options? I've also asked myself what are the positive things that being stubborn (or determined) bring to my life? For me, this soft approach makes it easier for me to accept some of those challenging aspects of my character. Now that I've reframed it, I realise that what I thought was a foible is actually one of my greatest strengths.

I'm also learning to dig into the energy behind the different words I use to describe myself. Yin Yoga is often said to teach patience, which is not a characteristic I can claim. To me, the energy behind patience is negative and makes me feel frustrated as I struggle to achieve something and need to do it over and over again until I get it right (or give up and ask Roger for help).

Instead, I believe Yin is teaching me commitment. I will stay in discomfort because I am committed to it and motivated to keep improving. The energy that comes with this is positive and encourages me to keep going, even when it's hard.

And my wonderfulness.

Hands up if you find accepting your strengths and wonderfulness harder than accepting your foibles?

I thought so. This is a challenge for me. When a new and good friend called me inspiring and some other wonderful words I won't repeat here, my initial reaction was to dismiss them and brush them off. Me, a shopkeeper's daughter from Yorkshire, how can *I* be inspiring? Then I paused and put myself in her shoes. She'd taken time and care to tell me of these wonderful things she sees in me. I know how frustrated I feel when the boot is on the other foot and someone dismisses or bounces a compliment back.

I then asked myself; what if I could be open to the possibility that her words might be true? And if they were, how would my life change?

Yes I know: these are big, challenging questions. I held on to that openness and the associated feelings for a few moments until they settled. I acknowledged that comments and opinions from others are only what the other person sees and I can believe them or not. My therapist suggested that I frame these as gifts that I can unwrap (or not) at any time. I like this idea too.

This time I decided I would believe them and I've stored them away in a corner of my heart to bring out in tough times. I've also decided that I am going to make them true. I will step up and own them.

And Now To Love

I absolutely wanted to be open to feeling more love but specifically, more self-love. This didn't seem British, and certainly was not something I was brought up to think about. You've already picked up how much I love Brené Brown's work and one reason is because everything she writes is born out of research. Reading her definition of love in *The Gifts of Imperfection: Let Go of Who You Think You're Supposed to Be and Embrace Who You Are*, hit me like a hammer blow.

A deep sense of love and belonging is an irreducible need of all women, men and children. We are biologically, cognitively, physically, and spiritually wired to love, to be loved and to belong. Okay, I agree. Then... *We can only love others as much as we love ourselves.* And if that wasn't enough *'practicing self-love means learning how to trust ourselves, to treat ourselves with respect, and to be kind and affectionate toward ourselves.*

Yes, I can hear you objecting too. Loud and clear.

If you feel the same resistance then you'll want to read these words from **Tracey Cleantis,** as she has a slightly different view. Her way into self-love is self-care.

I remember being asked – why did you want a child so much? It felt like the most ridiculous question, until I started to think about it more deeply. Why *did* I want it? The obvious reason (as well as a deeply personal one) was that I had not had the kind of childhood that I would wish for, for my own child. I wanted to give myself that experience. I realised I could do that. To answer the question probably the best place to start is with myself. If I'd had a child I would have been responding to *my* needs, to what *I* needed myself.

It made me aware that this was very much about trying to heal myself. That shifted me, and made me understand that I needed to start caring for myself. I need to be true to myself and not neglect myself in the way that I had been.

If you don't love yourself, the best way to get self-love is to engage in self-care. With honest actions of self-care you start to get to observe better. You consider, why am I treating myself this way? Notice how you're not being kind to yourself and even starting with, I'm going to do this nice thing for myself, I'm going to be responsive. Even if you're in a place of not loving yourself, you can move into self-love.

Self-love and self-care, one is a verb and one is a noun I suppose. Self-care is a way into self-love and self-love is a way into self-care. The more you do them, the closer you get to loving who you are, and the better you get at doing them.

The best way to start is to ask the question, 'if I were to treat myself like I would a close friend, how would I treat myself? How would I take care of myself in this relationship?'

Self-care has really allowed me to give myself what I so want; I am that responsive, loving mother to myself.

Self-Kindness

The key for Tracey is to ask the question, 'if I were to treat myself like a close friend, what would I do?' I'd like to tweak that a bit so it becomes;

'If I cared for myself in the same way as someone I love, what would I do?'

Ouch!

How do you feel when you say this?

Okay, we're on a roll, so let me ask you, how many times a day do you say things to yourself that you would never dream of doing or saying to those you love?

Ouch again!

Why being kind to yourself matters: some theory.

In the previous chapter you read about the mind/body link so you won't be surprised to read that being self-critical taps into your brain's threat defence system, the fight – flight – freeze response and releases cortisol and adrenaline. Your mind thinks it's under siege and reacts to keep you safe. It makes you stressed, anxious, and depressed and therefore not in a good state to achieve anything. This is great if you're being chased by a lion, but it's not very good in everyday life.

When you're kind to yourself and you react with a gentle touch or a soft voice, your body releases positive chemicals that calm you down and make you feel safe, accepted, and loved, therefore giving you a better chance of responding positively. Physical gestures remind you of caring emotions; they release oxytocin and lead to positive changes in your biochemistry.

So, the key to self-kindness is to talk to yourself in the same way as you would talk to a person you love and respect. I'll show you how to do that in the journaling questions at the end of this chapter.

If this feels like being bombarded by a hundred different reasons why self-acceptance is important, I make no apology. I agree with this quote from Cheri Huber, *Unconditional Self-Acceptance* (www.SoundsTrue.com). *The quality of our life is determined by the focus of our attention. Every life experience is shaped and moulded. In fact, it's created by our relationship with ourselves. All other relationships are a reflection of that primary relationship. Or, as we say, life is as good as your relationship with yourself.*

In the last chapter you read how I now have a strong mind/body link. The many ways that I nourish my body, are also where I am kind to myself. When I'm stressed I consider what will nourish me in this moment which encourages me to make more responsible and healthy choices for both my mind and body.

I've already written about the list of small pleasures I have behind my desk. Making time to do them is a way of bringing self-kindness into my life. It also reminds me that I am important and I always feel much better and relaxed afterwards.

Because of the work I've done I am much more conscious of how I'm feeling in any moment and act on it accordingly. I realise that being kind is about being strong and it brings balance to my life. Instead of pushing myself to do things when what I'm doing isn't working, I take time out for nurturing and a few minutes later I come back re-energised.

Helen Rebello has a different angle again. Making peace with the past and self-forgiveness was important to her.

To me self-acceptance means making peace with your journey, acceptance of everything that's happened to you, accepting that you're human, fallible, will have good and bad days, and that you might not always measure up to how you want to show up and operate in the world. And that's okay.

Peace, acceptance, and self-compassion are all intertwined for me. Things happened in the past that we didn't want, making peace with them has made us much stronger. We only have now. What's the point in putting your energy into the stuff you can't change; why not direct it into the stuff you can?

These are my tips for making peace with the past:

Start small, maybe pick one thing that you can focus on at any given time and work with that, for example not reacting to friends with children, and pick one small thing that you can change, that you can control. Accept that it's a journey but the point is not that you have to get anywhere with it. The journey is the point.

Every day you're moving forwards in some way, shape or form and when you look back over a few months you will see how far you've come.

Sometimes it's about where you put your focus. You really can enjoy every minute; you just have to treat yourself with kindness and compassion on the way and do what you need to do. Sometimes that might mean screaming into a cushion.

It's about giving ourselves permission to do whatever is right at that time and to treat ourselves like someone we love.

In many ways we're not kind to ourselves, and we talk to ourselves and beat ourselves up in ways that we would never do to someone we love. It's realising that you haven't done anything wrong and it's not your fault, and you haven't failed. Those are big things to get your head round. The biggest thing for me was that I felt like a failure.

You must focus on what you have, not what you don't have. As often as you can. It's not denying how you feel; it's noticing it and then choosing to shift it by not going down the rabbit hole.

Self-Forgiveness

Forgiveness is the only way to heal ourselves and to be free from the past.

Until we can forgive the person who harmed us, that person holds the key to our happiness, that person will be our jailor.

When we forgive, we take back control of our own fate and our feelings.

We become our own liberator.

Above is a quote from Archbishop Desmond Tutu in *The Book of Joy.* I get it, absolutely. But what if the person who harmed you is you? What if you are your own jailor?

I can absolutely see that self-forgiveness is good, and I'm very comfortable with what we did to try and get pregnant. Yes, maybe if we'd started trying for children sooner our lives may have been different.

One thing I've learned in both my NLP and Rising Strong training is that everyone is doing the best they can. Of course, if I'd known that my fertility was falling fast we wouldn't have waited so long, but I didn't, and we did the best we could with the information, knowledge, and resources that were available to us.

Think about it for a moment: do you do your best all the time?

Yes, I thought so.

Taking this into account could you forgive yourself for things you've done in the past?

For a moment, consider what's difficult to forgive in your life. What makes it so bad and what would happen if you did forgive or accept it? Or perhaps, what stops you from accepting it?

Now to Comparison and Judgment

Theodore Roosevelt said, *'comparison is the thief of joy'*. I certainly believe this to be true. In both the media and social media it's tempting to compare your *less than perfect life* with the *perfection* you see from others. It's very easy to gloss over any issues and believe that the grass is always greener. But you know that's not the case, don't you?

How many times do you look at 'happy' families and wish that it was you? For a while that was me, and then I realised that behind that perfection, many of our friends and family were really struggling with parenting, such as having children who won't sleep or are unruly. I bet you've got those sorts of friends too. Looking at their struggles really helped Roger and I to see that parenting can be very challenging. I can't count the number of times we've looked at others and been very glad that we're not in their shoes. We know that our grass is green enough.

The thing about judgement (so Brené Brown tells me) is that we judge people in areas where we're vulnerable to shame and we pick those who are doing worse than we are. This makes sense to me. If I feel uncomfortable about my body image I judge those who appear to be worse off than I am in some way. And the converse is true, when I feel comfortable in my own skin, there's no need to judge others.

This is a slow and gentle process for me. By starting with noticing when and who I judge, I aim to catch myself and if I don't that's okay. I also ask what might be at the root of my judgement and notice what comes up.

And now a different perspective, here's how **August** found her way in to self-acceptance by writing.

It was my Cognitive Behavioural Therapist who suggested I look at some of the online blogs for childless women. The thought terrified me, as at that time I was unable to discuss it without bursting into tears. But, over the course of a number of sessions and summoning up all my bravery, I dove in. It was thanks to the tools and techniques I learned on my Mindfulness course that this became possible, and I found myself on Lesley's site – reading the inspirational stories of other women and finally feeling able to look at my own pain, not be defined by it, but feel compassionate and kind towards it, and towards myself.

I have a newfound appreciation for the person that I am, just as I am, with all my flaws and foibles, disappointments and diversions. I now appreciate I wouldn't be the strong, resilient, compassionate, insightful person I believe I now am if these things hadn't come to pass – and therefore I have to be grateful for them, all of them – however hard those things were to live through at the time.

And finally.

I hope you now understand why self-acceptance is important and the different ways that you might approach it. I'd like to end with some timeless and wise words from Buddha.

You can search throughout the entire universe for someone who is more deserving of your love and affection than you are yourself, and that person is not to be found anywhere.

You yourself, as much as anybody in the entire universe, deserves your love and affection.

Absolutely.

Journaling Questions

- What are the key things you've learned from this chapter? Which areas would be helpful for you to explore? Examine these as you write in your journal.

- What strengths and wonderfulness have people told you about yourself that you find it hard to accept, and how would your life change if you believed them?

- How do you react when friends say lovely things to you? If your behaviour is motivated to deflect compliments, how could you change?

- How can you start to practice self-love?

- What self-care can you start? Make a list, maybe a list of small pleasures, and commit to doing one thing each day.

Self-kindness.

- What's one way you can start to be kind to yourself?

Here's a self-kindness practice.

Start with awareness. Notice when you're being self-critical, and listen for that negative voice in your head. When you hear the voice, bring to mind a close friend, someone you care for.

How would you react to them if they were in the same situation? Think about what you would usually do; maybe you'd give them a hug, or maybe you'd say something like 'don't worry, it will be okay' and notice how gentle, calm, and compassionate your voice is.

Now treat yourself like that good friend and see what happens.

*You may have to try a few different phrases before you get the right words, so experiment. You'll realise what messages are important to you and when it's vital for you to hear them. And if you're not yet sure what words work try these: **I will talk to myself the same way I talk to the people I love.***

If your natural tendency is to respond with a hug you can do that by crossing your arms and squeezing them tight, or by rubbing your arm. Try different ways and see what works best for you.

- Put a hand on your heart, breathe slowly and repeat a combination of these words either as a meditation, or at any time you feel stressed. Pick the words that feel right to you.

> *May I be:*
>
> *Filled with loving kindness, safe and protected, well in body and mind, strong and healed, happy, knowing the joy of being alive, live with ease and peace. May I accept myself just as I am.*
>
> *As you do so notice that you relax, and feel a sense of warmth, strength and courage flow through you.*

Self-forgiveness.

- Consider what if anything is difficult to forgive in your life. What makes it so bad and what would happen if you did forgive or accept it? Or perhaps, what stops you from accepting it?

Comparison and judgement.

- How do these show up in your life?

- For a few days, notice where you use judgement. Is it in areas where you feel less than?

  What would happen if you stopped?

Chapter Ten

I Am My Story – Putting It Into Words

I am the only one who can tell the story of my life and say what it means.

Dorothy Allison

There's plenty of evidence that writing helps in many different ways. In this chapter I'm going to focus on three – to help you recover from a traumatic experience, to gain perspective and understanding of what happened, and to tell your story.

In addition to my story and a selection of storytellers I'm also including the experiences of my good friend **Melanie Mackie** who had a devastating miscarriage a couple of years ago and wrote herself through the trauma using these three stages.

1. Expressive Writing to Recover from A Traumatic Experience

Research by Dr James Pennebaker (a researcher and pioneer of writing therapy) over many years concludes that writing about a traumatic experience for as little as twenty minutes a day for three or four days can produce measurable changes in physical and mental health. He called it expressive writing, and he meant to just write, let go, and explore what happened. Don't worry about spelling, grammar or punctuation. Just keep your pen moving continuously. Write from your feelings, so you're venting onto the page.

Here **Melanie** explains how expressive writing helped her through the trauma of her miscarriage.

I started writing a few days after the miscarriage. I was already familiar with what Julia Cameron in her book *The Artist's Way*, calls 'Morning Pages'. My notebook really became that outlet for me to say on the page what I couldn't articulate out loud or talk to my husband and family about, so it helped me to process what was happening.

It was like an anchor, I could sit and write about whatever came up, maybe some was ranting; whatever was going on is what came out on the page. And the great thing is that you can write freely. It's whatever comes, not self-editing, or withholding what needs to be written. Instead, it flows and comes from a place of free fall.

It was an outlet and it didn't upset friends and family. Your loved ones want you to feel better and you have to process grief in your own time and in your own way. People don't like to see you upset; it's distressing for them. My writing gave me that outlet where I could put down what I needed to without restraint and without upsetting friends or loved ones.

Each download is almost like having a chat with a really good friend. It's cathartic. My grief hit the page. I wrote as and when I needed to, stopping when I felt ready to stop. It was a way of life I already had and it served me very well during that time.

What Melanie describes here is writing to work through the initial stages of a traumatic event which also worked for me when Dad died.

2. A Regular Writing Practice to Process Grief

Committing to a regular writing practice can also assist in processing grief. In *Rising Strong*, Brené Brown found that when people wrote down their experiences of grief they were able to make it clear to themselves what they were feeling so that they could then articulate it to others. It was important to write freely, without having to explain or justify their feelings.

One way many people create a regular writing habit is what Julia Cameron in *The Artist's Way* calls Morning Pages. Melanie mentions it above. Each morning you write three pages of longhand stream of consciousness. As you might guess from the title of the book she suggests using them to regain your creativity; to me and many others they are so much more than that.

My Story: Accidentally Becoming a Writer

I kept a diary as a child, and after our Grand Canyon trip in 2004 I started a journal to capture all my thoughts and feelings. It was actually a cross between a diary and a journal; I wrote when I felt like it and included quotes and pictures. What I love is that it charts my life from 2004 to 2016 in three small books. I just took a break from writing to look through them, and interestingly the first one opened on the day Mum died. A few days later I started writing about how I was putting my feelings into a box. Hmm. I haven't written in this way for over a year and I miss it.

I spent most of my career writing contracts, so writing blogs for my website was a challenge. My wonderful business coach Karen Knott introduced me to Julia Cameron's Morning Pages and I've done these at least five days a week since. I wasn't writing when we went through IVF or the aftermath but writing did help me through my dad's illness and death.

I also agree with Brené that writing helps to process grief. It has been invaluable for me, especially since I opened myself to feeling. If you followed my suggestion to start writing when you opened this book, then I hope you're realising this too.

A safe place to be me.

I completely agree with Melanie that writing is a safe place for your darker side to come out, to really vent, rant, and just be you, knowing that no one will ever read what you've written. This is absolutely key; and I know many people who miss out on the benefits of writing because they're worried about someone reading it.

Melanie's point about writing what you can't tell your loved ones is also important. They always want us to be better, to not cry, and they don't always understand what we're going through. One of the really important things for me when seeing a therapist is saying what I can't say to family and friends, and writing is an extension of that. It's almost like having a therapist on hand all the time.

It took me a while to get into the habit of writing every day and there have been days when I've written a few lines of *I don't know what to write* or *keep the pen moving* and after a while I start writing more freely. Like any habit, it's important to keep going until you see the benefits.

Love answers.

For me, writing is like having an invisible friend, an alter ego, someone to talk things through with. I can vent my frustrations without upsetting anyone, and when I write about my challenges answers often emerge. I sometimes talk things through on the pages, 'if I do this, then that will happen, and on the other hand I could….' I aim to focus on my thoughts and feelings, and it gives me space and time to process challenging events from a safe distance and to gain perspective.

There's a point at which my writing becomes softer. As I understand it, your ego runs out after one and a half pages, then a wiser self, or maybe your true self emerges – I mean how long *can* you rant?

Here's **Melanie** again.

Once you've written a page or two your writing changes and you also get breakthroughs and epiphanies on the page. You get the initial splurge down on the page and then it becomes a lot softer, less angry. I would describe it as a download from a voice that isn't quite mine.

By nature I am reflective, and using the pages to process and consider events, comments people have made, what happened in my therapy sessions, and yoga lessons really helps me. It's also a place to celebrate my successes, and to explore why they happened.

Sometimes I ask for help, and pose questions such as, 'if love were in the room, what would she say?', or if not love, then a wise and loving friend (maybe even naming the friend).

A few months after Dad died I did writing course to help me through the grief process and I wrote several pages of longhand each day. There were prompts to write to which I found really helpful and using metaphors and stories helped me to process my loss. I've included a selection of prompts at the end of this chapter which you may find helpful.

Here's **Jessica Hepburn's** experience.

I found writing incredibly cathartic. I also really discovered that I loved writing and it's become a passion. For me it became a way of making sense of what I'd been through. The process of writing generally enables you to distance yourself from the process of living that seems to me to become quite useful in terms of grounding it, particularly if it's something painful. It's almost a coming to terms with that pain.

If you're trying to find a way to come to terms with the grief of unsuccessful treatment or involuntary childlessness, you have to do the work on yourself to make that okay. I think that work can take many forms. Writing is a way for some people to do this, and it is by no means the only one.

And from **August**.

> It was also during this process I began to use writing as a tool for self-exploration and self-acceptance. I had always written for myself, but it was Lesley's blog that inspired me to finally release my first piece of writing into the wild, for other people to witness. This new form of writing has introduced me to a new me, a more rounded, experienced and 'wiser than I knew' me – a new voice I didn't know I had.

When and how often to write?

I write a mixture of stream of consciousness and a diary. Maybe for me there's something important about keeping a record of my life, of what I felt and did. I confess that even after five years I find it hard to vent on the page, which is my nature generally. I very rarely lose my temper or vent my feelings so why would I be any different on the page? As I become more in touch with my feelings, my writing has changed too. I've had some big breakthroughs on those pages that have only happened because I'm committed to a regular writing habit.

In the early days I wrote three pages every day and now I write whenever I feel like it, and for how long I feel like, usually after meditating and before starting work. I carry my notebook with me and if something crops up that I'd like to record or *talk through* or to remember, I note it down. Sometimes I write several times a day, whenever I feel it would be useful to get something out of my head and on to the page.

Some people find it useful to download all their mental clutter as soon as they get out of bed, which transfers problems from their head on to the paper and empties the mind so they can concentrate on their day. Others write before they go to bed, which I guess does the same and clears the mind before going to sleep. It's like making a list, once you've written the list you can forget what's on it.

This is from **Pamela Mahoney Tsigdinos.**

> I write when the muse finds me. If it becomes an assignment you lose the organic nature of the writing itself. I have gone through periods when I don't write for weeks on end then I wake up one morning and write five pages. So it really does come back to – is there a particular experience, movie, conversation, or encounter that prompts you to think a little more deeply about something. They become exactly that, prompts.

The important thing is not to make it chore because then it loses its effectiveness.

Keep or destroy?

> **Melanie.** I generally don't go back and read my writing. Even before this I've burned old notebooks. There are several reasons for this: one, once it's out there I don't want to bring it back in to me if that makes sense. Also, I dread to think if anyone I'd written about read it later on. When you're really having an angry day or venting about someone, that is *not* what I would want them to read. It gives you freedom of expression when you know it won't be read by someone else and it allows you to write what wants to be said.

> The miscarriage was such a traumatic time that I don't want to revisit and it's a time I'll never forget. The burning of these journals was a spiritual practise in self-expression, getting out the trauma from within and releasing it from my energy so it reduces its impact.

For Melanie, burning her writing from after her miscarriage was a process of letting go of the trauma of the event. It's not unlike the ceremony I described in Chapter Seven.

I keep all my journals and find it helpful to look back and see how far I've come, maybe also because they're a sort of diary. Before I saw my therapist I'd set aside time to read what I'd written since the last time we met, which was a really helpful way to gain perspective on the week. In the same way, I sometimes go back six months or a year so I can see how much I've changed in that time.

Some of the storytellers told me that going back to read their diaries from when they were going through treatment felt like reading about a different person because they'd changed so much in the interim. It was also hard, as it reminded them of the pain they were going through at the time. Maybe re-reading is a matter of timing; perhaps more time needs to pass and more healing to happen before you can go back.

Here are a couple of points of view from our storytellers. First **August.**

> I burnt a great deal of what I wrote as a teenager and I regret it bitterly now.

One day I may want to revisit the journals I wrote when we were going through IVF to complete the healing process, to congratulate myself on how far I have come, and how much I lived through and the strength it eventually gave me. It is very challenging revisiting those things I wrote though, so I suggest caution to new writers before they decide to destroy what they've written.

Pamela Mahoney Tsigdinos has a slightly different view.

I have kept a journal most of my life because it is an opportunity to make sense of my day to day. Writing has always been an outlet and an opportunity to process. To make sense of things that didn't seem clear to me. As I learned more about the writing process, I understood that sometimes putting words to paper helps you visualise and understand things that are knocking around in your head but you haven't had a chance to sort out or put together.

I often go back and re-read what I've written. There are a couple of reasons. One is that on any given day you may think you understand something but as weeks and sometimes months and years go by you have the opportunity to revisit where you started and understand the progress, much of which is non-linear. You might take a few steps forward believing you'd figured something out but in truth you were still puzzling your way through it.

So my experience reading what I've written in previous years still gives me epiphanies. I still understand, yes, I thought I'd figured that out but I have more work to do.

My experience is similar to Pamela's but it came about in a different way. As I write this book, I'm digging into subjects and realising that, perhaps I could do some more work on this…. The important thing is to start writing then you'll experience the benefits for yourself, find a rhythm that works for you and think carefully before you destroy your notebooks.

In time I hope you'll agree with this quote from Martha Beck in *Finding Your Own North Star*.

Writing isn't just a task. It can be a confidant, a therapist, a good parent, a best friend, a channel to wisdom you didn't know you had.

3. Writing and Telling Your Story

The logical extension is to write and then share your story, and I understand how vulnerable and courageous this is. If I took a guess at what your inner voice is saying having read those words, it would be something like, *I could never do that*. When I was in your shoes I thought that too. Let me show you, through the stories, how this is a natural progression and how helpful and rewarding it is.

In Act One I wrote about owning your story and this is where we are now. To paraphrase the quote by Dorothy Allison at the start of this chapter, *you know that when you deny your story you allow other people to tell the story of your life and say what it means*. You've done enough work now to change this.

When I had a corporate job, I pretended I didn't like children so my colleagues treated me accordingly. In some ways it worked really well because they didn't expect me to look at baby pictures, and on the other I felt invisible and was gradually becoming more withdrawn and isolated.

We also didn't tell friends for several years and, as you know, keeping such a big secret can devastate friendships. You feel like they don't care. But how can they care if they don't know what you're going through?

Sharing my story publicly.

My experience of sharing my story could best be described as step by step and this is what I recommend for you. I know I have a website and book in my name loudly proclaiming my childless status, but it didn't happen all at once.

I've written about finding support by way of a group or therapist and I can't emphasise enough the importance of a safe space to open up. My storytelling experience started by talking to my friends in More To Life. Being able to talk to others who understood how I felt was a lifeline. In my conversation with **Beverley Glick** she emphasised the importance of having your story witnessed. This is what she said:

For a lot of people I've worked with, simply having their story witnessed by somebody they trust has been a major breakthrough for them. It can simply be someone you trust. I know Brené Brown talks about that, explaining there are certain stories that you should only share with someone that you trust. Having a safe space, with someone to listen, to witness and not to comment is very powerful and hugely healing.

Here's an example from **Linda Rooney** as to how writing and sharing her story on forums helped her.

Writing helped me a lot. The process of talking to and supporting other women (who were in turn supporting me) online meant that I was also able to accurately express my feelings, hopes, and fears. It meant that as I was writing to them, I was thinking through my situation, trying to make sense of what had happened and why I felt the way I did. It was a form of therapy.

I was lucky to talk to some very wise women, who were empathetic and insightful. Their thoughts challenged me, broadened my perspective, and crucially, taught me self-compassion. This self-compassion, something I'd never really indulged in before, helped me accept my situation, stop blaming myself, and opened me to consider the radical idea that my life could be good after all.

Over time, as I got stronger and more confident we started to tell friends and colleagues. Then I started a business, initially to coach midlife women, and in haste to decide on the name of my website I picked my name, which was a really big step in sharing my childlessness with the world. That business didn't work, because I wasn't being true to myself. In my heart I wanted to support childless women but I didn't feel strong enough to do it.

I wrote right at the start of the book how the shock of seeing Brené Brown's words galvanised me into action. I knew that I *was* standing outside my life looking in and it hurt. I decided that I'd had enough of hiding but I didn't know what to do;

being open and honest about my life and my story seemed too hard. So I did the best thing I could which was to ask for help. I found Karen Knott, a wonderful business coach who immediately believed in me and the difference I wanted to make in the world. Her belief and the work we did together gave me the courage to show up and let myself be seen.

A couple of years later I worked with **Beverley Glick**, who helped me to make sense of my whole life and where infertility fitted into it. When I looked at my life from above I could see patterns I hadn't previously been aware of, which showed me that many issues I thought were related to my childlessness began much earlier in my life. Knowing this enabled me to put my childlessness into the context of my whole life.

As I got stronger inside, I became prepared to tell more of my story. I wrote on my website's first About Me page that we had *too many* rounds of IVF, and two years later it said *six*. Originally writing six felt too much to share, maybe I felt ashamed but now it's okay. That's my story and I'm comfortable telling it. There's obviously more I could write; however, it's Roger's story too and my boundary for this is now set.

I've been asked whether there's any situation where I wouldn't be happy to say that I'm childless and my answer is 'no'. There are obviously many occasions when I don't say it, but the decision is mine and I feel comfortable talking about my life anytime. That is my wish for you.

Enza Gandolfo wrote a novel based on her experience.

Writing my novel *Swimming* helped. As a writer, my primary mode of making sense of the world is through writing. The whole time I was struggling with infertility, I was writing. Sometimes this was very personal journal writing, sometimes it was more structured academic writing, sometimes it was fiction, but all my writing helped me to work through my feelings and to think about the way womanhood and motherhood are linked in our society, and the way childless women are perceived.

When I realized that I probably would never have a child and decided to stop trying to get pregnant, I felt an overwhelming need to do something with the experience. In some of the worst moments, knowing I would one day write about the experience gave me hope. I felt there was so much silence about miscarriages and infertility and that being able to tell my story – through a novel – was one way of breaking the silence and contribute to other women's lives. It was also a way of challenging the stereotypes.

Writing *Swimming* was about imagining an older woman, not me, and her making a life without children. Writing it was painful at times but it helped me work through many of the issues I was facing. And now when other women read it and tell me their stories, and tell me that reading *Swimming* helped them, I feel I've made a difference and I've made something useful out of a painful experience.

Johanna Walker told her story publicly at a storytelling event. Here's her experience.

> I was at a summer camp for girls, seeing mothers dropping off their daughters. The pain of grief was seething through my body because I would never take my daughter to summer camp. And I could not bear this pain.
>
> That was the day I opened my journal and decided to write it all down. I remembered the quote by Isak Dinesen, 'All sorrows can be borne if you put them into a story or tell a story about them.' I wrote everything down. I told the story. First in the chamber of my heart, then behind closed doors in circles of trusted friends. Then I heard a talk by Jody Day. What a relief to hear her story. Because she spoke, I am speaking now. That's how we open doors for others. Because I showed up for the grief with my whole body and heart I transformed it into something else. Story creates a container in which we can bear what feels unbearable. It helps us find our place in the world. We get to reframe it and to rewrite the big story of who we are and who we get to be.

Here's **Melanie** again.

> I felt very strongly after my miscarriage that I would share and write publicly when I was ready and it took over a year to do so. Our friends and family knew I was pregnant but not everyone, so it was a bit like the elephant in the room and I needed to address it. Also, through sharing our story and putting it out there I wanted to pay it forward and help others; like the other women and couples who shared their stories and helped us. That was very much a driving force.

Once it was published I did have quite a major wobble in feeling: *this is out there now*. And that was quite difficult to overcome. I don't know what it was that made me feel uncomfortable. Afterwards it was very liberating. But at the time it was tough to go through.

It's about letting the grief unravel in time, which is individual. It's about being ready, and it takes inner strength; we have to do the grief work before we can share our stories. For me, telling my story was part of my healing process, acknowledging that it's part of my life and my story. Accepting that I'm in this club and I didn't want to be.

What will people think?

Putting your story out in the world in your own name is a *big* step and for various reasons several of our storytellers have used a pseudonym or just their first name. Others felt it was important to be seen. **Pamela Mahoney Tsigdinos** wrote a book about her childlessness and has a blog, both in her own name.

I thought very much of writing under a pseudonym but I thought that for it to be meaningful to other people they had to attach it to an actual human. To say I'm willing to be candid, vulnerable, open, and honest with you about the sheer pain and suffering that women like us have experienced. I challenge you to feel that with me and to try to understand how you as a reader would have reacted under those circumstances.

So did Jessica Hepburn.

Publishing a book in my own name felt like a very big thing for me. I'd been very private and secretive, and my book is very honest. I was really conscious that everyone in my world knew who I was.

One of the things you have to accept is that especially when you give them this painful information is that they won't always react in the way you expect or want them to react. You have to try and hold that and protect yourself within that. Some people you're not that close to will behave in an extraordinarily empathic way and others who may have been through the same experience, and you thought you were really close to, don't behave in the way you hoped. But it was an overwhelmingly positive thing. You can say if you really want to understand me, read the book.

The book was a really good way of exploring those feelings and to let people understand them if they wanted to. The other thing it's done in many of my relationships, particularly with those people I'm close to, is that it's not an elephant in the room. We live with it in a way that feels very open. And hold it in a positive way; people are now less worried about hurting me.

Melanie had a similar experience with friends.

Who steps forward and who steps back was a huge thing for us. By sharing our story people stepped forward who maybe had gone through it themselves, or who knew someone who had and really showed us amazing support, so that was brilliant. And unexpected.

What was hugely disappointing for me, and may be for you, is there are others who will shy away from it, and they can be people who are your closest friends or who you've known a long time, or just cannot handle seeing you in a different way or hearing what's happened. They will choose to avoid it. For me, that has been a big part of learning about grief and us as human beings, whether it's through whoever we've lost, what it does to us and the trauma, and connecting with other people's stories that are really powerful.

It doesn't matter who we are in life, we're all going to suffer loss at some point and shying away from it is not the answer. But we don't have control over how everyone reacts. What we do have control over is our own reaction to it, and for me it was building that self-resilience to cope with that.

It's difficult to say whether you're ready to tell your story openly or not because it's not a definitive line. But you accept this is your life, so it becomes part of your story and accepting your life isn't what you wanted it to be but this is who you are and this is what's happened as a result.

My own experience of sharing my story has only been positive because by the time I had this website most of my friends and family knew we were childless. They didn't know the details or how we had struggled, and asking them to read a blog was easier than talking to them face to face. The overwhelming response has been one of empathy and compassion. You've already read how sharing her story really helped **August**, even though that isn't her real name. I also know that my blog was the first place **Helen Rebello** told her story openly, and she had empathy back in spades, which has given her confidence to be more open about her story generally.

I've told my story or parts of it many times now. At the start it was hard and took every ounce of courage I possessed, but now it's easy. I'm involved with The Story Party which holds events in the UK where you can tell a personal story, to a theme, for ten minutes, and without notes. I've told different aspects of my story twice. The hardest part was remembering everything, and both times there have been friends (and Roger) in the audience who didn't know what I was going to say. It was amazingly cathartic and uplifting and afterwards, several women told me that they or someone close to them struggled to get pregnant or is childless. By sharing my story I helped them to feel less alone.

This has been my experience so many times when I've spoken to other women. Having a miscarriage, finding it hard to get pregnant, and not being able to have children is common, and by sharing my story I have given others permission to own theirs.

Reluctantly becoming a writer.

The final rung on my writing ladder (for now anyway) is writing this and (she takes deep intake of breath) calling myself a writer. There are several times in my life when I've made a quick decision, jumped in with both feet, not really considering what's involved. And writing this book is one of them.

Following my decision to write, I found a book coach, made a plan using coloured pens and post-it notes, and became excited when all the storytellers said yes and sent me additional contributions. It was all going really well.

Until it wasn't.

Until there were gremlins shouting in my head phrases like *you can't do this, this is hard, what you're writing is no good.* You get the picture. I tried various techniques to shut them out of my head but they wouldn't go away. I asked for help and at the same time started my private yoga lessons.

I can honestly say that the coaching sessions and my personal yoga lessons I had at that time changed me more than anything else I've ever done and in a short time the gremlins left and enjoyment came back. Writing has encouraged me to be more open and vulnerable, to write things I've never previously voiced out loud, all of which has taken my healing to a deeper level. I've learned an incredible amount from the storytellers and digging into each chapter has encouraged me to question what I'm doing and why. Of course, it has been really challenging at times, but I can honestly say that I've loved (almost) each moment and I'm so glad I answered the call.

I have had wobbles since, most recently when we confirmed the publication timetable. My first reaction was excitement and I might have said a few words I couldn't possibly repeat here. The next morning everything changed as reality sank in. This is it. This is it now. It's actually happening. I'll soon be holding my book in my hand. These words I've written here at my desk could soon be read by anyone in the world.

This was a *very big thing* and changed me fundamentally. Many tears were shed as I started down the road to acceptance. To accept that I will be a published author not just in my head but with all of me, my heart and body. It took some serious meditation, journaling, and yoga to get me back to myself.

I'm sure there will be a few more wobbles leading up to publication. Like everything though, knowing the reason I'm writing and operating in a way that meets my values are key for me. I have changed so much in the year of writing, and if I help others then that will be amazing.

Journaling Questions

Now I'm not suggesting that you write a book or have a website or blog in your name, but I would like to encourage you to start a writing practice and then in time to write your story so that you can truly own it. Here are a few ways for you to start.

- What are the key things you've learned from this chapter? Which areas would be helpful for you to explore? Examine these as you write in your journal.

- How could you start a writing practice? Could you commit to writing in a journal (or electronically) every day for a month? If you're worried about others reading it, how could you address that? Could you shred your writing each day, or delete or password protect what you've typed? Experiment with different practices and see which works best.

- What other questions could you include in your writing practice? For example 'Today; I will …' 'I am looking forward to …', 'I am grateful for…'

- What about writing your story? How could you start to do this?

- What would you need to take one step forward, to share something small with one person?

- What about sharing on a forum, or blog? You could start by using a pseudonym.

If you're finding it hard, here's a selection of prompts to get you started.

- What I love about myself.

- What I'm really proud of.

- The best thing that happened today/this week/month/year.

- What holds me back.

- I'm excited about…

- How I've changed in the last year.

- A dream I have.

- The last thing I celebrated.

- The best decision I made this year.

- I am challenged by…

  And some to write through your grief.

- Who I was before I was childless.

- If I could tell my story (what would change)?

- If grief/sadness had a voice, what would it say?

- The same for kindness, self-compassion, or love.

- What would it take… (for me to let go of what's holding me back, to lean into my grief, be open to new possibilities)?

- What does my heart (or soul) want me to know?

- Look at the quotes I've used at the start of each chapter and write to one of them.

- How have I changed…. (since I started trying to be a mother, since I started reading this book)?

- Imagine your life in a year, in five or ten – what do you see?

- How has this changed me?

- If I could love and accept myself, then…. (What difference it would make). Use this question for each chapter (for example, if I could connect to my body…).

Chapter Eleven

You Don't Have to Do This Alone – Finding Your Tribe

Anyone can show up when you're happy. But the ones who stay when your heart falls apart, they are your true friends.

A A Milne from Winnie The Pooh

Let's go back to when the realisation you weren't going to be a mother started to creep into your bones. You believed you were completely alone. You ventured onto the Internet and your heart dropped into your feet as you entered *childless* into the search engine. You found some people like me and other bloggers who said they've been where you are and for a moment your spirits lifted. Then as you read more you realised they are writing from a completely different place and you found it hard to believe that they were ever where you are now.

You signed up to their newsletters and read their blogs, but commenting was completely out of the question.

After a while you became more courageous or were perhaps fed up of being stuck. You explored a couple of forums and maybe even commented, but not in your own name. Maybe you started to open up a bit and it felt very safe because it was easier to tell strangers about your struggles than to tell friends.

There was something missing, though. You wanted more. You wanted to sit across a table with other women who've been where you are, because until you look into their eyes you won't ever really believe that anyone else understands what you're going through.

This is when you need a support group.

And before you read more, please give yourself a pat on the back, because if this is you, congratulations, you've come a long way already. And if you're not quite ready, that's okay too.

As you've probably worked out by now, healing is a process. You start off hiding from the world and even from yourself (especially from yourself) and then, over time you start emerging, slowly, slowly. In safe places. In the forums you gain confidence to be yourself, and you start to feel a spark of your inner strength coming back. It's only when you've gained enough strength that you feel confident to talk to people face to face.

Why a Support Group?

There's something really special about sharing your story with people who understand and can tell you that 'you're not alone', 'yes, I had that experience' and most importantly 'I used to feel like that and now I've moved on'. Mostly it's knowing that you can share your story and challenges in a completely safe space and others will understand.

For me this is one of the things that make a support group special. In the following stories you will read how important joining a group was for me and the four other women who wrote about it, then we'll discuss in more detail what their experiences have in common.

My Story: How Joining a Support Group Saved My Life

Joining a support group saved my life.

I don't say that lightly.

After finishing treatment, on the one hand Roger and I felt numb, lost, and isolated, and on the other we were relieved that it was all over and we could move on; if only we knew what that moving on would be.

All our friends had children and we had no idea how we were going to make new friends who understood us, or where we'd find them. We went into hibernation, not really connecting with anyone and we felt very alone, like we were the only people in the world who were struggling. After about a year we summoned all our courage and reached out to the local More To Life group. They were planning a day trip from London to Cambridge and we decided to go. Until then we didn't know anyone else who was childless and all of a sudden we were about to meet fifteen others. This was the days before social media so we had no idea what to expect or what they looked like. The plan was to meet at Liverpool Street station. We bought our train tickets and decided that we'd check them out from a distance before committing ourselves. They looked okay, just like normal people, so we decided to join and it was the best decision we've ever made. Without doubt.

I remember feeling like I'd just hit the jackpot. Here were a group of people who, even though I was meeting them for the first time, I felt completely at home and comfortable with.

Because they saw me. They knew what we were feeling, and they welcomed us with open arms. We talked, laughed, and empathised, and when we got home we *knew* that we could be okay.

That was fifteen years ago and in that time a number of the women and couples have become our closest friends. We turn to them in hard times because they 'get us' like no one else. We are there for each other when our hearts fall apart and when we're happy. We have supported each other through divorces, job changes, a wedding, and many of us have lost parents. I believe we have unbreakable bonds. Yes, some of us are closer than others, but we know we have friends we can turn to who understand us completely.

Women's or couples' group?

For us it had to be a couples' group. It was important for us both to meet other couples in the same boat and to grieve and heal together. There have been many times we've met and the men have been in one place taking about cars, gadgets or something along those lines, anything but the thing they have in common. Meanwhile the women have been in a different room, or sitting at a different table, talking about our feelings or challenges. Over the years we've grown immeasurably and the talk is more general now, and deeper.

If there had only been a women's group available, then I guess I would have attended, but I feel it would have separated us as a couple as I found others to talk to and Roger didn't. I don't think our marriage would be as strong as it is had we not joined More To Life together.

I met **Jill Duffin** on that trip to Cambridge and she and her husband are two of our closest friends. Here's her experience.

I was fortunate that More To Life (MTL) was just starting. Over the next few years this was a lifeline for me. As well as reading the newsletters and looking at the forums, I gained a lot from meeting others, and we have formed some really strong friendships. Although we all had different stories to tell, I knew I was in a safe environment where anything could be discussed.

From **Liz Asham**.

The most important aspect of being a member of a support group for me is the friendship and understanding I get from the other members. Our regional group is very close. We meet up regularly and I have formed some very close friendships as a result. I don't know how I would cope without them or the group and thank my lucky stars that I discovered it.

A safe environment, friendship, and understanding were key for Jill and Liz. For **Christine Bishop** it was knowing others who were in the same place.

I did see a couple of counsellors which helped a little, but the main help was knowing that others were experiencing the same feelings and emotions as we were.

While we were at an infertility conference we had listened to a talk from a More To Life Member. It was so good to know that not everyone comes out the other end of fertility treatment with the longed for 'miracle baby' and that those who don't were getting on and leading fulfilling lives.

> Not the lives that they would have wished for but fulfilling nonetheless. We joined up and it was a real lifeline for me. We went to some get-togethers and have made lifelong friends through the organisation. One couple became our closest friends, more like family in fact.

Linda Rooney has a slightly different perspective, that of being in an online group.

> I was fortunate to find a very supportive group of women from all over the world on The Ectopic Pregnancy Trust website based out of the UK. I live in New Zealand, and it was wonderful to connect with women from Ireland, the US, Australia, India, or Canada, and to support each other.
>
> On a message board, writing and thinking about our experiences and emotions, we supported each other through (often) multiple ectopic pregnancies and losses, and our efforts to conceive after that. Some of us went on to live lives without children, and it was good to have companionship and understanding as we came to terms with that. Having someone to talk to – whether it is in real life or online – really helped me feel less alone.
>
> Online groups also offer a degree of anonymity, which can be comforting when you're questioning everything about yourself and your confidence is at an all-time low.

Joining a group is a big step and **Louise** only joined after she'd exhausted all other options. She also demonstrates what I wrote earlier, that first we meet people online before we gain the confidence to meet face to face. From an early beginning as one of the 'oddballs' sitting next to her at the Christmas meal, Louise is now one of my closest friends.

At the beginning of 2003 I decided to join More To Life. Anyone who joins knows that their hopes and dreams have been shattered and there will be no children for them. It sounds miserable and for a long time I refused to join, as in my opinion, support groups were just for lost causes and no hopers. When I hit rock bottom, had cried on the shoulders of all my friends and family, all of whom had children and could not imagine what it was like to be childless, however hard they tried to for my sake, MTL seemed like the only option left.

MTL was the answer to my prayers. People simply understood me without me needing to explain things. For the first few months, I met people over email. I eventually asked the local representative to come to my house to meet me. The thought of trying to meet and cry in public was too much. My sister worried about me inviting a stranger into my home at a time when I was so vulnerable. That had not occurred to me. I was simply desperate. I didn't know who this person was, if they were a trained counsellor or, if my sister was right, someone who would prey on me when I was at such a low ebb. The worry was unnecessary and Judy was, and still is, simply one of life's wonderful people who listened, shared her experiences and took me as I was. By the time Judy left that evening I knew I could survive.

Eventually, I plucked up the courage to go to my first group face-to-face meeting, a Christmas meal. The deal I made with myself was that I could leave at any time. Simply going was a big step and another stepping stone in my recovery. I deliberately sat at the end of the table so that I could leave easily. In my heart I expected people would understand the pain I was feeling and how hard joining the oddballs would feel.

I was right. From the first meeting I felt at home and at each new meeting I found yet another person who would say 'I used to feel like that, I know what you mean, oh not you too!'. There was so much that we shared. MTL was exactly the place I needed to be. Over time I gained courage to write articles for the newsletter and to respond to posts on the online forum. Writing was cathartic (as writing this is) and was my chance to repay the kindness others had shown to me.

Through MTL I've made some lifelong friends who enrich my life in a very different way from when we first met, raw with pain and no interest in the world. If you asked any of us now about the reasons for each other's childlessness, I doubt we would be able to remember as it is no longer the glue that binds us together in the way it was when we first met.

The silver lining from the infertility cloud is the close group of friends I would never have met if life had followed the plan I wanted.

'Support' group or a group of friends: what's the difference?

I've used the term 'support' here and certainly we got a lot of support from each other, but there was no 'official' support or help. We were a group of friends finding our own way. We all wanted to find our way, we read books together, attended workshops, and helped each other whenever we could. A major role was to witness each other's stories, without judgement or wanting to fix it, which was incredibly healing.

There have been others we've known over the years who left after a while because they wanted to stay stuck. Maybe we didn't voice it overtly, but we were moving on with our lives, make no mistake.

There are dangers in groups too, especially when the dynamic is one of wanting to stay stuck or of revelling in being the victim. You know those people I mean, who get a lot out of being a victim. I wrote about this in Act One and if the whole group (or the 'leader') views themselves as a victim then my advice to you is to find another one.

What if I can't find a group?

Maybe you're throwing your hands up in the air because you've searched the Internet and there are no face-to-face groups near you, or there are only women's groups. Then this could be time to take your courage in both hands and either actively look for others and maybe set up your own group, and/or to seek professional help.

What about friends you already have?

The chances are there are women or couples already in your life who don't have children. A friend told me recently that she met one of her closest childless friends at work and another on a training course.

It's also useful if you can, to find older women and couples, as role models, who have had full, interesting lives without children. Roger and I are pleased to have this role for our friends' children, who can see by our example that they can lead a full life whether or not they have children.

Asking for Help – When The Support of a Professional Helps

I grew up believing it was weak to ask for help and it's taken me until recently to change that. I realise now that asking for help is the strong action to take. However, in the UK there's a lot of stigma attached to it. I mean we're happy to employ a plumber or accountant so why not ask for help with our feelings?

I've spoken to many women who've had no help at all and lead a great life, and others who wouldn't be where they are now without some form of help or working with a therapist. There's no magic formula here. What's clear though (as you've no doubt already discovered) is that you can't talk to friends and family about this because they don't understand. Being a member of a support group can help and sometimes only a professional can provide what you really need. I'm going to throw in some caution here too; I also know that finding a therapist who you can work with can be a challenge too. In *The Next Happy*, Tracey Cleantis includes some great advice about how to find a therapist. Over and above that, my recommendation is to see at least two before you decide.

My Story: From 'Do I Have To?' to 'I Love It!'

I've already written about how I was the perfect description of 'keep calm and carry on'. Until I couldn't. In addition to getting upset at what seemed like trivial things, snapping at Roger and feeling sad, I would often wait until I was in the house alone and then allow myself to cry, or just sit staring at the computer screen. Eventually after another incident, I reached out to my good friend Karen Anderson, a therapist in Las Vegas who facilitated the workshop I attended based on Brené Brown's book, *Rising Strong*. The conversation went something like this:

Me: Karen, can you help? Can you make any suggestions, please?

(What I was really saying: you started me on this path to feeling and it's harder than I thought it would be so do you have a magic wand or a book I can read to make me feel better?)

Karen: You might find it helpful to talk to and work with someone.

Me: I have a big resistance to seeing someone as it feels like failing and there's a stigma about 'needing' to see a therapist. I feel I should be able to do this on my own.

(What I was really saying: Noooooo, and f***. Am I so messed up that I need to see a therapist? I'm an only child, and we don't like asking for help. Surely there's a book or two I can read that will help. And, I'm British. We don't do therapy here.)

Karen: It seems that you're in the heart of the myth of 'I can go it alone and I can opt out …' but the vulnerability and courage is in the asking. The workshop we did was intense group therapy so you've already experienced it.

Me: Okay I trust your judgement and I surrender, as an only child we have a tendency to believe we can go it alone and I realise that this time I need help.

(What I was really saying: Do I have to? Really?)

And after a while… Okay, okay I give in reluctantly, I'm really miserable now and I've had enough of feeling like this. I've asked for help before and it's worked out pretty well, so why not give it a try. Worst case I can go once, I don't have to go back.

So I *reluctantly* went to see a therapist and it was the second best decision I've made. I would've loved this to be Karen but she's a friend (and lives in Las Vegas). Instead, with her help I was led to work with a woman who is also an only child without children, both of which made me feel validated, seen and heard, and in her office my healing *really* began.

I'm not going to list all the positive changes that I've made since that day; suffice it to say that I've made more progress since then than in many years before. I guess it was the right time; I'd got to rock bottom and had enough of feeling very low. I certainly wouldn't be writing this now without her help and she has been a catalyst to making many other changes.

The key things I've gained from talking to a professional are:

- It's the only time you get to talk about you knowing they will listen without judgement.

- They will make suggestions of things you can do to help, small or large changes.

- They will normalise what you're going through. I remember the relief I've felt many times when she's said, 'oh don't worry about that. It's normal'.

- It's a completely safe space. You can say anything you want and show any emotion that comes up.

- And most of all, they have no emotional connection to you and (unlike everyone else in your life) their only interest is you.

Here's **Helen G's** experience of working with me.

> In May 2015 I heard the Woman's Hour programme on IVF and the BBC Radio 4 programme 'Drawing the Line'. I heard Lesley talking about More To Life and looked up the website, which then led me to Lesley's website. This was a complete revelation to me and tears rolled down my face as I read all of the amazing inspirational stories. For the first time in 12 years I had at last found other women whose experiences, feelings and pain mirrored mine. Gradually, through doing the Let Go and Move On programme, starting to read some of the many books available on this subject and looking at blogs, I've developed a better understanding of the grief and indeed recognise my childlessness as a bereavement and that all the feelings I've had and still have are ok.

Journaling Questions

- What are the key things you've learned from this chapter? Which areas would be helpful for you to explore? Examine these as you write in your journal.

- Search the Internet to see what groups are available to you. Are you ready for an online group in your area or would you prefer face to face?

- If there aren't any groups available to you, maybe start by commenting on a forum before you suggest meeting up with others in your area.

- Consider working with a therapist. In the UK the British Infertility Counselling Association has details of therapists who specialise in infertility and childlessness.

Chapter Twelve

Notice What You Have, Not What's Missing: The Importance Of Gratitude

The mind is everything. What you think, you become.

Buddha

It turns out that human brains have something called a negativity bias, where we focus more on what's 'wrong' than on what's good in our lives. Sometimes we hang on to these negative things for months or years, all of which can make us more pessimistic, anxious, and at the extreme, depressed. At the same time we hardly acknowledge the things that go right. Does that sound familiar? Or maybe it used to and as you're working through the book you're starting to turn the tide?

The bottom line is that what you focus on determines which pathways in your brain connect and therefore strengthen. This in turn determines what your brain pays attention to in the future, so if you focus on pain, worry, stress, regret, etc., you'll have more of these in your life. Of course, the opposite is also the case. When you focus on positive things you become more resilient, optimistic, grateful, and happy.

Not sure? I know you're familiar with this because before you started trying for children, you never really noticed babies, and then all of a sudden they were *everywhere*, and now every time you look up you see 'happy families.' Am I right?

If you're still not sure, try this. Think of an item, maybe a bag, coat or pair of shoes you'd really love to own, or (perhaps easier if you live in a city) a particular model and colour of car. It has to be something you've never really noticed before. For the next few days, as you go about your life, be aware just how many times you see it.

The good news is you can change this negative bias and I'm sure you don't need me to tell you that you do this by focusing on positive things. One way to do it is by having a gratitude practice. Yes, I can hear you sighing and saying things like *not that again* and before you jump ahead to the next chapter, please bear with me, as there's plenty of research to back me up.

Why Gratitude?

Professor Martin Seligman, the father of positive psychology discovered that having a gratitude practice is one of our most powerful mood elevators. Since his discovery, there's been plenty of research which demonstrates that those with a daily gratitude practice are happier and have higher reported levels of alertness, stronger relationships, enthusiasm, determination, optimism, and energy. In addition, they experience less depression and stress. A gratitude practice also builds resilience to help you get through challenging times, and it enables you to bounce back more quickly from adversity.

Are you convinced now?

Having a gratitude practice also enables you to shift your perspective away from what is missing in your life towards what you have. In other words, moving from counting your burdens to counting your blessings.

In Act One I wrote about how you have the right to choose your mindset, and this is the same. You have the choice whether to view every moment as a gift and therefore to have a life of rich opportunities or whether you'd prefer one of sadness and misery. To quote Brother David Steindl-Rast, an Austrian Monk and expert on gratitude and joy: *You don't have to be grateful for everything that happens in your life, but you can be grateful in every moment.* Having a gratitude practice will help you make that shift.

Have I persuaded you that a gratitude practice is at least worth a try?

I get it, I'm grateful. Is that enough?

I'd love to suggest that you say 'I'm grateful' three times, spin round in a circle, and your life will be changed forever, but we both know that's not going to happen.

Having a positive attitude is helpful but you need more than that.

I'm very convincing when I say that I have a healthy eating attitude. I know exactly what to eat to be healthy, and I have a shelf of healthy cookery and exercise books. But what good are they unless I practice? What good are they if I ignore them and eat a bar of chocolate? It's only by practising regularly that I become healthier.

The same is true of gratitude: an attitude will get you started but it won't get you the positive benefits I mention above.

And one more thing: once you have a gratitude practice, you'll find that you start to look for things to be grateful for, therefore enhancing your life even more.

My Story: Realising How Grateful I Am

When you're in the mire of grief, everything can seem bleak. Sometimes finding one positive thing can start to turn the tide. When my dad was terminally ill, I was really struggling and everything seemed grim. A good friend suggested that we work through the book, *The Magic* by Rhonda Byrne, which is essentially a 28-day gratitude workbook. Doing the exercises in it every day meant that, just for those few moments, I focused on something that was positive in my life instead of what was negative. Having the practice and the daily check in really helped me especially as Dad died during this time. I have mixed feelings about the book itself; however, it did encourage me to start a nighttime gratitude practice which continues today.

Even though my biggest dream didn't come true, I've always realised that there was more in my life than being a parent. I haven't forgotten what's happened to me and, with the various practices I've learned, I've been able to put it in context and focus on other things. Of course, this didn't happen overnight, and it was a combination of changes, including my daily gratitude practice.

For me, having a gratitude practice and consciously choosing to do things that bring me joy really go together. This combination has made my life much richer. Now, when I complete my gratitude practice at the end of the day I have many things to choose from, and overall I feel a lot happier in myself and with my life.

Here's what **Johanna Walker** says.

I have a daily gratitude practice that reminds me to cherish the life I do have, the life I am living. Practice is just that: practice. That means sometimes I forget, for sure, and get caught up in judging my life and wishing it were different. But the practice is to honour and cherish the life I am living. Without that, it's like cutting off limbs from my own body—the harshness of the criticism I have heard inside my own head ('Your life isn't good enough. Your life isn't as good as that other woman's. You are not a whole woman' etc.) is violence against myself. Gratitude is the best antidote to this.

Specifically, it's pretty basic: each morning (or each evening, if I don't get around to it in the morning) I make a list of three things I'm grateful for. Usually the things I notice are the little things. A friend who has done something thoughtful in my direction, a really good breakfast, the feeling of my bare feet on grass, that I get around mostly by bicycle. Like that.

I also have what I call a 'flash practice.' This is just that: any time during the day when I notice myself getting grumpy or down or discouraged or judgmental of my own life, I pause for a moment and notice what's around me. No big drama. Just a split second recognition of the beauty of my life. This helps. The more I do these flash practices, the more the thinking gets recorded in my mind, and the inner critic/harsh judge has less power, because the compassionate voice of gratitude is becoming much stronger.

> Sometimes it's not even a 'thing' that I'm grateful for. But it's a felt sense. I just pause and notice gratitude. It's a feeling in my heart that is humble and clear. OKAY. My life isn't perfect, but thank God for my life. Exactly as it is.

I'm convinced. How do I practise gratitude?

It can be as simple as looking around at what you have to be grateful for, and seeing what happens. I'd like you to start by noticing that, even though your biggest dream didn't come true, there are many, many things in your life to be grateful for. Think about it for a moment. You were able to buy this book (and you can read it). The chances are good that you have a roof over your head and enough food to eat, which means that you have a far better life than many women in the world.

This is not to negate or minimise what's missing in your life. Focusing on gratitude and what's positive in your life is an extension of the Letting Go process I wrote about earlier, because it will let in new and more positive feelings.

Journaling Questions

- What are the key things you've learned from this chapter? Which areas would be helpful for you to explore? Examine these as you write in your journal.

There's only one. Start a gratitude practice and commit to it.

- A great way to get your gratitude muscle working is to pause now, set a timer for ten minutes and write down as many things as you can think of. I challenge you to write at least twenty.

- Habits take root when you can see the benefits and this usually takes around a month, so start simply with something that fits easily into your daily schedule. Experiment with the different ideas below and see which works, be flexible and most of all *commit*. And when the month is over, carry on.

1. Every day in your journal write down three things you're grateful for today and why. I suggest that you do this in the morning, so that you start the day with a positive mindset.

   Use something like this wording: *today I am grateful for/truly blessed to have/happy and grateful for* .... *because*.......

   If you're not sure what there is to be grateful for in your life, think about your health, your body, work, finances, friends and family, nature, your house, and any other things you have in your life.

2. Find a small stone or crystal that fits comfortably in your hand, maybe from a place that's special to you.

   Keep it by your bedside.

   Last thing at night, hold it in your hand, think about your day and answer this – *What's one thing I'm grateful for today?*

   It could be anything, what's the first thing that pops into your head? Then say thank you.

   Doing this means that you'll search through all the good things that happened and in doing this you may find several things to be grateful for. You'll also end the day in a positive frame of mind.

Even if your day might seem to have been negative, something good has happened. You could also say thank you for one thing that made you laugh, and one thing you achieved today.

I love this, my stone is from one of my favourite places, Malham Cove in the Yorkshire Dales. I find it a really helpful way to end the day.

3. If you want a variation on this, you could write your one thing on a piece of paper and put it in a jar. Then you'll have a record of gratefulness you can dip into if you're feeling sad.

I use a variant of this process to record my successes and achievements. Once a year I empty it out and am always surprised by how much I've achieved.

4. Another variation on the stone option is to keep one on your desk, and every time you see it, touch it, pause and say *I am grateful for*.... whatever pops into your head at that moment.

5. If you have a meditation practice, meditating on the positive things in your life also works. Spend time visualising all those things you're grateful for, and notice the positive feelings that arise in your body as a result.

6. Use your daily writing practice to write about those things you are grateful for. Or even better, about those people who have made it possible for you to be who you are today.

A couple of suggestions.

There's a school of thought which suggests that if you consider the reason you're grateful for something, you'll feel it more deeply so end your thanks with *because* .....

Taking a moment to pause and really feel the gratitude and positive feelings in your body really helps to rebuild those new pathways in your brain.

Seligman and other researchers suggest having a daily practice, and I certainly recommend this to start with and after a while, play with what works best for you.

Chapter Thirteen

Yes, You Can! Reclaiming Happiness and Joy

*Tragedy breaks down your door and takes you prisoner. To escape
takes effort and energy.*
*Seeking joy after facing adversity is taking back what was stolen
from you.*
Option B: Facing Adversity, Building Resilience and Finding Joy

Sheryl Sandberg and Adam Grant

Every sentence of this quote resonates deeply with me. For
many years I felt like I was a prisoner, hiding myself in a sad
place, safe behind walls I'd created. I'm guessing this was you
too. I write *was* deliberately because if you've worked through
the journaling questions, by now you'll be starting to see that it
is possible to have a fulfilling life without children, so in this
chapter we're going to take the next step and reclaim happiness
and joy.

If this feels too much for you at the moment, I completely
understand but please read on anyway with an open and
curious mind. As with all the chapters I know you'll learn
something, and maybe you will surprise yourself.

What Is Joy And How Is It Different from Happiness?

It's fair to say that you could tie yourself up in knots researching both these subjects on the Internet. Some writers use both words interchangeably, while others state that they're different. After chasing down a few rabbit holes myself; here's what I've concluded.

1. Joy is deeper than happiness. It's a way of being in the world and it's closely linked to having a gratitude practice.

   To quote Brother David Steindl-Rast, from his book *Gratefulness, The Heart of Prayer*, '*Joy is happiness that doesn't depend on what happens.*' As you might guess from the title of his book, he (and other researchers) have found that having a gratitude practice is the bringer of joy into our life. I would also add that (along with grief) joy is one of the hardest emotions to feel.

2. Joy comes to us, not by searching for extraordinary moments, but by celebrating the ordinary moments in our lives.

   Think about it for a moment. What are the most joyful things that have happened to you recently? Were they big things or small moments? Two recent examples for me are feeling completely relaxed when I was having dinner with a couple of friends and being in the countryside, grass under my feet, blue sky above, and feeling the wind in my face. Both were completely ordinary moments.

3. I'll be happy when…. is a myth. Happiness is not linked to having things.

There's plenty of evidence proving that having more things doesn't make you happy and, as I've written, being grateful for what you have is the way in. Think about it: when you buy something new, how long does that initial rush of happiness last? It's not very long, is it?

4. Suffering can be integral to joy.

    In her book *Finding Your Own North Star*, Martha Beck explains how we can feel intense joy as a result of pushing through pain and to get to this you have to accept your life, in all aspects, including the suffering. One of her students writes, *I realised that by accepting my sadness and then going beyond it, I could find a deep source of happiness inside myself, one that will be in my life as long as I am.*

    This resonates with me completely. When I think back to moments when I've felt intense joy, many have come after I've pushed myself really hard and done something I didn't think I could.

5. They're both feelings, and you can feel them now.

    Way back in Chapter Six I discussed grief and wrote about feelings. Since then, I hope you've been learning to feel. As you've experienced the dark emotions, you will have noticed that you're starting to feel more of the lighter emotions too. And, like any feeling you can feel them right now. Here's how.

    Think of a time when you felt really happy, a specific time. Now go back to that time. Feel what you felt, see what you saw, and hear what you heard, including what you were saying to yourself. Sit in this experience for a moment or two. And when you come back, know that you can go back to this any time you want to.

6. We want more of both in our lives.

    Whether you believe happiness and joy are the same or not, I'm sure you'll agree that you want more of them in your life. So let's create some. And for ease I'm going to focus on joy.

How to Bring More Joy Into Your Life

You've probably worked out that there's only one way, and that is to work out what brings you joy and do more of it.

Before you throw your hands up in horror, I do realise that's a lot easier for me to *write* than it is for you to *do*. Perhaps think of this as an opportunity to explore, to discover more about you and what you love to do. Like many voyages of discovery, you may have a few false starts along the way and perhaps your endpoint could be more interesting and (yes) joyful than you ever imagined.

Here are six ways to generate some joy in your life and at the end of the chapter are some suggestions to get you started.

1. What are you curious about?

Maybe you've heard people saying that you should follow your passion or purpose. Well that's all very well if you know what they are, but most of us don't.

As you've probably worked out by now I love Elizabeth Gilbert and in her book *Big Magic: Creative Living Beyond Fear*, she advises forgetting passion and instead following curiosity. She explains that passion can be a dangerous impulse as it takes everything from you, whereas curiosity only gives. It asks, *is there anything you're interested in?* It could be anything, large or small and it only has to capture your attention for a moment. This is a clue, and she advises turning your head a quarter of an inch and following it. Follow it a bit. If it really grabs your attention that's great, and if it doesn't, let it go, ask the question again and follow something else.

Following different clues may lead you nowhere or it may lead you to your passion but as she says, *'You might spend your whole life following your curiosity and have absolutely nothing to show for it at the end – except one thing. You will have the satisfaction of knowing that you passed your entire existence in devotion to the noble human virtue of inquisitiveness. And that should be more than enough for anyone to say that they lived a rich and splendid life.'*

Amen to that.

A tiny spark of interest in gardening eventually led to her writing the book, *The Signature of All Things* and, as she says, *'this only worked because I said yes to every single tiny clue of curiosity that I have noticed around me.'*

2. Do something creative.

Being creative is another way to bring more joy into your life and it can also be a challenge to embrace. As children we are extremely creative until the point where either shame or comparison steals our joy. In *Daring Greatly*, Brené Brown says that 85% of the men and women she interviewed *'could recall a school incident from their childhood that was so shaming, it changed how they thought of themselves as learners'*. Approximately half of those were what she refers to as *'creativity scars. They could point to a specific incident where they were told or shown that they weren't good writers, artists, musicians, dancers or something creative'*.

Hmm, I've certainly got those. I can't draw or paint, so I have big art scars and others from cookery lessons where the teacher was terrifying and nothing I produced was ever good enough. As I write, just thinking about both art and cookery classes puts me into shame and I want to hide.

Is that you?

I used to have a narrow definition of creativity and, because of my lack of art skills I believed I wasn't creative. A few years ago, I shared this conclusion with a friend and she was aghast. 'But you have a business, you write, you're a great cook, you take fabulous photographs. Okay maybe you can't draw, but that doesn't mean you're not creative.' I reluctantly agreed with her, and so began the scavenger hunt to find my creativity which has brought more joy into my life than I ever thought possible.

3. To play or not to play.

Another way to find joy is through play. The National Institute for Play in the USA lists plenty of research that demonstrates how play transforms personal health and relationships. The founder, Dr Stuart Brown, describes play as a *state of being*. He says that it is *purposeless, fun, and pleasurable* and we do it because we want to. It's also an experience, not a goal. That seems right to me. Imagine for a moment animals playing, and notice how much joy they feel.

Play will also be different for each of us; the key is that it has the characteristics mentioned above.

4. Feel more of everything.

I've already been encouraging you to feel more, and especially not to shy away from grief. As you feel more of the dark emotions, you'll also be feeling more of the light. This has certainly been my experience. I was recently hit by a wave of grief and for a few weeks after I'd processed it, so much joy kept bubbling up that I had several bouts of unexplained laughter.

5. Make someone else happy.

Think of the last time you did something small for someone else. Maybe you gave a small gift, or a gesture that helped them in some other way. How did you feel in the moment? And remembering it now, you can still feel that glow, can't you?

Apparently, this is called *giver's glow* and was named by Stony Brook University School of Medicine Professor Stephen Post who discovered that even the anticipation of giving releases the feel good neurotransmitter dopamine. This has been known for centuries. St Francis of Assisi included '*it is by giving that we receive'* in his Prayer, and many of the world's religions encourage followers to give.

I've only recently come across this and it makes complete sense; you'll read in a moment how much joy giving brings to my life.

Smiling at others is another way of making others happy. There are many health benefits to smiling, so why not do it more often? And even better pass a smile on to someone else.

6. Look for it.

Now this might seem obvious, and as I see it, it's a mindset shift in the same way as having a gratitude practice. It's about consciously noticing those ordinary moments and appreciating the joy in them.

My Story: A Scavenger Hunt for Joy

After Mum died it seemed that all the joy had been sucked from my life and a big turning point for me was joining a choir. I've always loved singing and was in the choir at school. Since then, other than singing along to songs in the car, it was confined to hymns at weddings and funerals.

It took me a long time to find the right choir and going to the first few sessions on my own was a real challenge for an introvert. However, I can say now that it brings more joy to my life than just about anything else. And it's so much fun. Being in harmony with others is beautiful and we make a far better sound than I could ever imagine. At the core it's about being in the moment, feeling the music, the words, and how the emotions resonate throughout my body. I've also made some lovely new friends, yes, some of whom have children or grandchildren, and that's okay, when we're singing we only have one purpose and nothing else matters.

It also ticks the giver's glow box for me big time. We have many concerts, some to raise money for charity, others to bring joy to the audience. One of the most memorable was in the dementia ward in a hospital. Remembering the joy we brought to the patients that day fills me now with a warm glow.

Recently, I've been consciously considering what brings me joy. I've already written about my list of small pleasures, small things I enjoy and how doing at least one each day has added small pockets of joy to my life.

I've been looking back at what I used to love to do as a child. One of those was hand sewing. I decided to finish a couple of tapestries Mum had started and something strange and wonderful happened; once I started being creative, I couldn't stop. Tapestries seem like a winter project, so in the summer I started making felt lavender bags and I absolutely love the whole process; from creating the designs (as long as I don't have to draw), picking the colours, sewing, and giving them to friends. In a world where many tasks we do are never ending, sewing gives me a sense of achievement and pleasure that I'm often missing. There may be inconsistencies in my sewing and that's okay. I get a lot of joy from what I create and in the end, that's all that matters. Another benefit is that when I'm sewing, it has my complete attention so anything I'm worrying about is put aside for a time.

I also used to love embroidery so bought a kit. I have no idea whether I can still do it, or if I'll enjoy it, and that's not the point. I'm curious about it and that's all that matters. Together with my childless friends, we've held craft days where we each bring a creative project and spend time together working on it and chatting. The original idea was, as we don't have children, we don't generally do as many creative things, so why not? They are great fun and an opportunity to learn from each other.

This curiosity also leads me to Yin Yoga and my experiences bear out Martha Beck's conclusion that pushing through a challenge brings joy. Those sessions that have pushed me hardest and where I've achieved something I never thought I could have brought amazing joy. I also realise that following these experiences I have a burst of creativity, which both soothes me and integrates my learning.

My yoga practice is also helping me to *feel* more. In the chapter on Grief I explained that when you numb the dark feelings you also numb the light. I notice that now I'm leaning in to those darker feelings, I've also been feeling so much more happiness and joy and have had several bouts of hysterical giggling. One was at the start of a Cranio Sacral Therapy session. My therapist and I were both laughing and then I just couldn't stop for what seemed like ten minutes. The best thing is I have no idea why I was laughing. Just like grief, there was some joy inside that wanted to emerge, so I allowed it. I've had the same experience in my yoga lessons; again I have no idea why, especially as I was in discomfort at the time.

If you imagine emotions range in intensity from zero to a hundred, I used to go up to a maximum of maybe plus and minus fifteen. These days that range is so much bigger and is extending all the time as I continue with this work.

I'm consciously taking time to stop and pause and look for the joy in everyday small moments. For example, I just took a break from my desk to make a coffee. As I was waiting for the machine I looked out of the window into the garden, I noticed a busy blackbird, the beautiful Acer turning red for the Autumn; I heard the wind chimes which reminded me of our travels and I recalled times we'd sat in the garden with friends. I remembered the shop where I bought my mug and spent a moment really savouring the taste of the coffee. The simple act of making coffee brought many small moments of joy, because I paused. It didn't take any time out of my day. I was doing what I always do; the difference was my mindset. As a bonus, I came back to my desk refreshed, feeling like I'd had a long break.

Giving to others brings me a lot of joy. Making a difference is one of my core values but that's not it. I get an incredible amount of joy from small acts of kindness, taking a friend some flowers, sending a helpful email, asking someone how they are (how many people don't do that?), making business introductions, taking time to say how much I appreciate someone, making someone laugh, or organising to meet friends.

When I think back over the past week, and those times where I've given, I do indeed feel that giver's glow and where I feel it the strongest is not when I've spent money, but when I've given a few moments of my time, myself, or my love.

For me, joy is like gratitude in that having a practice is more important than an attitude as it encourages me to search for joy, which in itself brings so much more into my life.

I've read that learning flows from our heads to our hearts through our hands, and maybe that's what I'm doing now. I've gone through a lot of changes in the last couple of years, and maybe sewing and yoga are ways of integrating them and taking them to my heart.

In conclusion I agree with Elizabeth Gilbert when she says, *'I am going to spend as much time as I can creating delightful things out of my existence, because that's what brings me awake and that's what brings me alive.'*

Here's how some of our storytellers answered the question, 'what brings you joy?'

Johanna Walker. Playing with children. Because I've done so much grief work, my heart has opened up in big ways, and there's a lot more space and much clearer attention for young people. I am like Mary Poppins. I have been close to my niece since she was born. Now she's 18 and I'm the person she calls when things get hard. I'm the person she writes about when she has to write about a significant person in her life. We are soul mates. I have 10-year-old twin niece and nephew and being their ally and wrestling with them and being their punching bag for all the hard stuff is a huge joy. I'm super close to the 5-year-old daughter of a friend and when we greet she holds me and doesn't let go. This all brings me great joy.

Growing flowers. I stand in my garden or at my kitchen window and just watch the flowers grow. This brings me daily joy.

Doing my work. Helping people tell stories. Helping people speak. When someone comes in with an ache, knowing she has a story to tell and is too scared to tell it, or too scared even to dig it up; that I get to help her on this journey is a profound honour and joy. To witness the story come to life is breathtaking.

Being comfortable in my body, at 52.

Rosalind Bubb. Dancing, music and art have been incredibly important to me. I felt as if Ceroc dance, and my community of adult friends there, was one of the things that kept me sane. (Ceroc is a fusion of different dance styles and it is easy to learn, sociable and fun. It can be danced to any music with a regular beat.) I love being part of an orchestra and several music groups, and I enjoy all sorts of arty activities in the evenings and at weekends. It's one of the benefits of having a simple, childless life. I make the most of it, and I really enjoy it.

Tracey Cleantis. Looking back and seeing the certainty in which I clung to thinking that I couldn't imagine happiness without a child, I am flabbergasted by all the joy, passion, and happiness in my life. I find particular joy in working as a therapist, writing, speaking with others, and helping those who are struggling get to the other side of their pain to their next happy. I love being able to share all that I have learned with others and give them hope and assurance that you can be very happy even if you didn't get what you most wanted.

August. Both my husband and I feel we have a duty to make the very best, most fulfilling life that we possibly can. It would be a waste, and ungrateful, to not throw our everything into making the fullest life possible for ourselves.

I gain joy from writing, from learning, from travelling, and from spending quality time with the new me, and the people around me that I love. These passions will fill my future more than adequately. I intend it to be very, very full.

Helen G. Things that make me happy are walking on a beach looking at the sea, listening to birdsong, watching things develop in the garden, spending time with people who inspire and encourage, and the feeling I get when I've helped someone or done something special for someone.

I decided recently to list all of the things I would have liked to have done with my children and maybe just do them where possible. For example, I would have enjoyed doing craft-type things, so I volunteered to help at a children's activities morning. I've also recently rediscovered my enjoyment of knitting and sewing. Finding a creative outlet has been important both in terms of expressing myself and feeling the satisfaction of creating something. Another thing I would have enjoyed doing with my own children is reading to them and hopefully encouraging them to enjoy books as I did as a child and still do now. I have started volunteering at my local school, hearing children read. It's part of a reading recovery scheme, so I'm working with children who need some extra help and encouragement and I'm enjoying being in that nurturing role and building up a one-to-one relationship with them.

> I have happy memories of watching children's films as a family on winter weekend afternoons, so this was also on my list. Although I would feel self-indulgent doing this on my own, I was treated to a viewing of *Frozen* on a visit to friends whose daughter was a fan and I really enjoyed it!

I find the range of things listed above to be extremely interesting, and hopefully they've given you some ideas of things you could try for yourself.

What might get in the way.

Joy can be hard to feel because it requires you to be vulnerable and to open up and, let's face it, it's just not British. In *Daring Greatly*, Brené Brown introduces the concept of foreboding joy, where thinking things like, 'this is too good to be true, how long can it last' stops you from fully feeling joy. I didn't understand this until recently. One day I was feeling really joyful, realising how much I love my life and the adventures I'm having. Before I could enjoy those wonderful feelings, into my head popped the words 'but how long will this last?' and as a result the joy quickly dissipated.

The answer, Brené says, is gratitude, so if you experience this, acknowledge how grateful you are for whatever it is that that brought the joy. Doing this enabled me to soften into the moment of joy and feel it much more both at the time and since.

To conclude with a few words from Shonda Rhimes from *Year of Yes: How to Dance it Out, Stand in the Sun and Be Your Own Person:*

'... maybe you're paralysed because you have no idea what your passion is. The truth is, it doesn't matter. You don't have to know. You just have to keep moving forward. You just have to keep doing something, seizing the next opportunity, staying open to trying something new.'

Absolutely.

Journaling Questions

- What are the key things you've learned from this chapter? Which areas would be helpful for you to explore? Examine these as you write in your journal.

Here is a selection of ideas to help you to find your joy.

- Think back over the past month. What experiences have brought you joy? Write them down, and notice what (if anything) they have in common. Do more of them!

- Make yourself a list of simple pleasures, and commit to doing at least one each day.

- In the next week commit to doing something that you wouldn't normally do that reconnects you to yourself; paddle in the sea, walk barefoot in the grass, sing and dance to loud music, roll in the snow, have a water fight. Notice how it feels and do something else next week.

- What makes you really laugh hysterically? Do it.

Curiosity.

- What are you slightly curious about? What are you a tiny bit interested in? Commit to following your curiosity for a week or a month and see where it takes you. If you discover you're not really interested in it, that's okay, start again.

Creativity.

- Now do the same for your creativity.

- What did the ten-year-old you love to do to be creative? Do it.

- Do something creative that you haven't done for a while; bake, sew, paint, colour in, take photographs, write. Follow Elizabeth Gilbert's lead and explore gardening.

- Learn something new or expand your skills and stretch your comfort zone.

Play.

- What do you absolutely love doing, where you forget time? Do it.

- Take yourself back to your ten-year-old self. How did that girl play? What made her laugh, and what did she love doing so much that she forgot the time?

- How can you do that now, or if not the exact same thing, the essence of it?

- Do this for other ages. What did the seven-year-old, twelve-year-old, fifteen-year-old you love to do?

- Make a commitment to put aside fifteen minutes a day to either play or to be creative.

Feelings.

- Have you noticed that, by letting in grief and sadness, you're also feeling more joy?

Generosity.

- Make a list of ways you can give a moment of your time, yourself, or your love to others. Pick one and do it.

- Start smiling more, maybe as you travel to work, or in the shops.

- Savour and enjoy every moment of the giver's glow.

Small moments.

- Actively pause and look for small moments that bring joy into your day.

- Then notice how different you feel after taking the pause.

- If you feel the shudder of foreboding joy, notice what's happening. Firstly breathe; breathe in and out to a count of four or five, and when you feel calmer, shift to practicing gratitude. Start by saying 'I'm grateful' a few times then expand to 'I'm grateful for.....', perhaps in time with your breathing. Then when you're calmer, lean in and feel the joy.

And whenever you feel joy, remember to write about it in your journal.

Act Three

Learning to Fly

Introduction

'It's the end of the world' said the caterpillar. 'It's just the beginning' said the butterfly.

Unknown

When you opened this book, you were struggling to come to terms with your life, and now, having read the different stories and worked through the questions in Act Two you can see that there is light at the end of the tunnel. And it's not a dim light; it is a *bright shining light,* so let's take a few more steps forward and grab it with both hands.

You are different now. Think about it, a butterfly is unrecognisable from the caterpillar it once was. It looks and behaves in completely different ways. Now you *might* not have changed quite that much, but everything you've worked through in Act Two has changed you.

This Act is about exploring those changes and learning how to incorporate them into your life. In butterfly terms you are working out what colour and shape your wings are, and at the end you'll be tentatively starting to fly.

It is in two parts, firstly we'll look at who you are now and then move on to what you might want to do with your life now and in the future.

Chapter Fourteen

Becoming Yourself

I was never going to become anything but myself.

Patti Smith

In Act One, I wrote about values and you made a list of your core values. I also quoted both Pamela and Louise who said that they're fundamentally the same as they've always been. I've also found that to be the case and perhaps you will too. As you've been through this work one or two of your values may have changed or maybe the emphasis has shifted a bit.

My Story: At the Core I Am the Same

Since learning about values in my NLP training, I've reviewed mine every year or so. Mostly they've stayed the same; making a difference, authenticity, courage, and growth have been constant. In the last year, since my personal growth has accelerated and I've been writing, there have been a couple of changes. This reflects how different I am now. Or maybe my current values reflect who I *actually* am, not the armoured up person I pretended to be for many years.

Journaling Questions

- Go back and re-do the values exercise in Act One. You may find that they are all the same, or some have changed. Whatever the case may be, it is absolutely perfect. Keep this exercise close, as you'll be using it in the next chapter.

- What are the key things you've learned from repeating the exercise? What has changed and what's stayed the same? Explore these as you write in your journal.

Chapter Fifteen

Yes, You Are! Stronger at the Broken Places

The world breaks everyone and afterward many are strong at the broken places.

Ernest Hemingway

Kintsugi is the Japanese practice of repairing fractures in porcelain with varnish or resin powdered with gold, silver, or platinum. Each piece looks different and is unique. The scars form part of its history and add to its beauty. It is also stronger and won't break in the same place again.

So it is with us.

Recognising How You've Changed

By now, you've read many stories so you know that each woman was 'broken' in different places and that she put herself together in her own unique way.

The suggestion that I too might be repaired with gold came to me when I read Tracey Cleantis' book *The Next Happy*, and it seems obvious. What you've been through has brought out both the best and the worst in you and through it you will have discovered some qualities you didn't know you had.

If you're not sure what I'm talking about, here are a few examples:

Lisa Manterfield. I'm stronger and more compassionate than I was. I really understand how people can be carrying around huge hurts and I'm much tougher and more willing when I see someone needs help through a difficult time. At the same time, I've become timid in many ways. Something I once believed could never happen to me did happen to me and it's sobering.

Jessica Hepburn. I am fundamentally the same person but I also believe that all our life experiences shape us. I think everyone in the world is dealing with something that hurts them. My hurt was not being able to have my own biological child with the man that I love but the key to life is about making up for the sad and the shit things. If there's one single thing that's different about me now than in the past is that I understand and embrace that, at a deep and profound level.

Helen Rebello I am confident about who I am and what is important to me – and I am much better at taking ownership of that. I am hugely spiritual which gives me acceptance, clarity, and peace. I live as much as possible in the present and I have changed my mindset over the years to embrace blessings and face the fear of challenges – I believe we all have the resources to deal with whatever comes our way, even if we don't always know it at the time.

Tracey Cleantis. I still have the wound of this loss; I always will, it will never go away, yet it no longer hurts as it did. Now I can actually say that I am truly happy that it all worked out as it did. Five years ago I could never imagine saying that, much less having it be my real truth. And that *is* my truth.

Christine Bishop. I am a very different person now than I was before. For a long time after the end of our treatments, I thought that without a family I could never be happy. But I am now in a much better place in my life. I have realised that everyone has their own cross to bear, and even those people who on the outside seem to have everything and be living a perfect life are often not happy and have their own problems to face.

August. I am a more balanced, self-aware, self-loving version of me. I have learned more about myself going through these hard years than I think I ever would have without them, and though I certainly wouldn't want to relive the pain, I am grateful for the wisdom and insight it has eventually brought me.

It has also created a profound level of understanding between my husband and I. We have had the most unbelievably difficult times and conversations, things I am not sure a lot of couples would have come out the other side of. And though our relationship did incur damage through our experiences, our emotional connection and understanding is something else – something special and unusual – something we feel blessed to have.

Jody Day. I genuinely believe that going through the grief of childlessness has had a profoundly transformative effect on me as a person – for the better. I am kinder, more patient, more compassionate and more empathic with all who suffer. I have a greater sensitivity towards all disenfranchised groups now that I have firsthand experience of what it feels like to be part of one. Childlessness has also made me braver – I've lived through my worst nightmare and survived, so I know how resilient I am! I've also learned that I couldn't have made it on my own without my childless peers, so I'm also more willing to be open and vulnerable with others; I am both stronger and softer.

Enza Gandolfo. I feel stronger and surer of myself and less concerned about what people think about me. Less put out by questions about whether I have children or about why I don't have children.

Grief is a strong emotion and one we don't talk about enough. Most of the time, I don't think about my childlessness. Some days, especially when my friend's teenage children are being particularly difficult, I am grateful that I am childless. Thankful even. But some days, holding a newborn or sitting around at a party with a group of mothers talking about their adult children, about their grandchildren, the grief returns, intense and painful. It doesn't last long, but it's there. I don't think this is a bad thing. We miss and grieve for those who are lost to us; it is part of being human.

Louise. Along the way I have learned life can be tough; some things are just not meant to be; to expect the unexpected; to rise every time I fall, and never to ask the question 'do you have children?'

Cali Bird. For me, it's a profound gift of happiness. When I was in my late 30s I never expected still to be single and not have had children. I went into my 30s like that and found myself going out of my 30s. My scary age was 43. If I can't get this sorted by the time I'm 42, biologically I'm pushing it. I thought how am I going to cope, how will I survive. But when I did get to that age, we were together in a solid relationship and I didn't have kids. But it was really happy. I could never imagine I would be content to be so happy. So that gift for me is the gift of a deep happiness that came about by not getting what I thought I wanted.

Linda Rooney. I'm so much more in touch with myself now, my emotions, my talents and yes, even my flaws. I also think that my infertility and loss has tempered me, forged me into who I am today; someone who is wiser, kinder, more compassionate, more realistic, and yet more optimistic too; someone who is contented, happy. Someone I like.

Jill Duffin. This quote has been my motto since I read it in *Crossing the Moon* by Paulette Bates Alden, *'Maybe it's possible to get to a place where what is best, is simply what is.'* I am grateful that I have a partner who loves me for who I am and that our marriage has gotten stronger. I am also very grateful for the strong friendships we have with other childless women/ couples.

> **Liz Ascham.** I've learned a lot from my experiences and have gained strength and compassion. Life is hard and we don't always get what we want, but we have to make the most of what we do have and focus on the positives. I try and focus on what I have and not on what I don't. Having said that, I do believe that it is important to acknowledge our sadness about the life we hoped for and not be afraid to talk about it.

That's a really interesting selection, don't you think? To me it demonstrates our individuality.

My Story: Learning to Be Me

For many years after we finished IVF I stumbled along not really thinking about things, getting on with life in my Yorkshire way. Looking back, I now realise just how numb and empty I was during that time.

I'm very different now. I guess the bottom line is I feel so much more comfortable in my own skin. I hardly recognise the younger Lesley; yes at the core she is the same, and over the years many of her wonderful characteristics became hidden. Working out who I am, who that authentic Lesley is has been a process of uncovering these and using them in my life. As you've read, much of this happened more recently as I dug deep into the different subjects in Act Two.

Writing this book has been a wonderful catalyst and this past year has been a head, heart, and soul journey. At times it's been a bumpy ride, but I've loved it and am glad I had the courage to answer the call.

Learning to grieve has put me in touch with my emotions and, for the first time in my life I *feel* so much on the inside and I know how to express emotions on the outside. When uncomfortable feelings come up, I know I can't fix them, so I sit with them and allow them to pass.

I've let a few layers go and I'm getting closer to my authentic or true self. As I get to know her I realise that she embodies all of those wonderful words that others have used to describe her. Switching my thinking to accepting compliments instead of batting them back is a habit that will take a while to fully embrace. It has changed me so much and accepting my 'wonderfulness' means that I feel much more confident.

Mum always called me *stubborn* and maybe I am sometimes, and reframing this to *determined* sits so much better with me and encourages me to keep going when things are tough. I also realise how strong I am, another word that I never previously claimed. I always thought I needed support and I do function better in a crisis with Roger by my side, but goodness me I've been through a lot and I'm still standing, well more than standing. I'm jumping up and down with joy at the fabulous life I have.

The biggest change has been the relationship I have with my body and how it is now leading my mind. Letting go of limitations and expectations on the yoga mat encourages it to do so many new things which is very exciting and each time it does, another belief I had about what I can or can't do is shattered. My body now tells a story of strength, power, and achievement. The deep connection I now have to my heart means that I am kinder and more compassionate and more understanding of both mine and other people's challenges.

Both my curiosity and creativity have become energised; I've tried many new things, found that I love some things I used to do and I have a list of others I want to explore.

One of the biggest changes has been letting go of outcomes. Throughout my life I had to have a plan, with a defined outcome. Maybe what's changed is learning to trust. For example Emma, my yoga teacher, has a plan for me, and I don't need to know what it is because I trust her implicitly. I've also learned to trust myself more, especially my instinct so when my inner self says 'write a book' I follow it, without knowing what I might do afterwards. In the past, just the thought of not knowing would have caused me to panic, and now I'm perfectly relaxed about it. I guess being more relaxed is another way I've changed.

I am so much more in touch with myself and life. It's as though all my senses have been turned up; there is a lot more happiness and joy in my life and so much to be grateful for.

Maybe the biggest change is that I have a deep, *deep* inner peace and calmness, which grounds me and it's like all the work I've done this year has brought me home to me.

As I end this part of my story I realise I haven't mentioned being childless. I will always be childless, in the same way that I will always be an only child who has lost both parents. Because of the work I've done, I can confidently say that all of these have shaped me, but none of them define me.

Journaling Questions – Who Am I?

At the end of these questions your aim is to have a really good idea of who you are now. There are several parts and at the end you'll bring it together perhaps in a creative way.

- Looking back over my story and the other stories in this chapter you can see how we changed, so spend some time reflecting on how you've changed too. What positive qualities do you have now that were previously hidden from you? What strengths do you have now?

- Also consider what you've learned about yourself as you've worked through this book. Maybe go back over each of the chapters in Act Two and read your journals and notes. Reading my story above will also help.

- Take a sheet of paper and write I *am* on it in big letters. Now fill the rest of the sheet with all the positive words that describe you. If you have a set of coloured pens I challenge you to write each word in a different colour and keep going until you've used them all. Think about the qualities you have, especially the new ones that you listed above, and words that others have used to describe you. It may take a while and you could always ask friends what they see in you (something I personally find challenging).

Here's a selection of words to get you started: strong, compassionate, kind, understanding, confident, comfortable in my own skin, spiritual, more balanced, self-aware, self-loving, less concerned about what people think, more in touch with all of myself, more realistic, optimistic, contented, accepting of what is, curious, creative, courageous, caring, supportive. And I 'm sure you can think of plenty more.

Here's a short meditation to help you to get in the right mindset:

> *Sit quietly. Feel your feet on the floor and your body as it touches the chair.*
>
> *Breathe in to the count of four, and out to the same. Notice the space between the in breath and the out breath. Do this a few more times and feel the air going right into your belly.*
>
> *Once your body and mind are still, ask the question 'who am I?' Drop the question into your body, and notice where you feel it.*
>
> *If any feelings are stirred up, notice them and let them pass.*
>
> *When everything is still, drop the question in again. Notice what words or feelings come into your being. Write them down.*
>
> *Maybe do this a few times over a few days and notice what different words and phrases come to mind.*

This is me.

Now let's bring these together.

- You have the sheet of paper with I am on it, and you also have the results of your values exercises. Your aim now is to consolidate them into one document that describes you. Make it as creative as you want. At the simplest, use a sheet of paper and some coloured pens, and if you'd like to be more adventurous, maybe cut out images from magazines or cut and paste them from the Internet. Perhaps include your photograph in the centre. Do whatever feels right to you. The most important thing is not to judge. No one else needs to see it.

Keep it somewhere you can see it. I have two copies, one pinned to the board behind my computer and the other in my journal. I look at them regularly and they make me feel really confident and positive.

Chapter Sixteen
What Story Are You Telling Now?

There was another life I might have had, but I am having this one.

Kazuo Ishiguro

In her story, Jessica Hepburn introduced me to the above quote and it sums up this final chapter, my life, and the lives of the other women here.

In Act One I wrote about story and how when you own your story, you can write your own ending. This is where we are now.

If you've completed the questions in the last chapter, you'll have a pretty good idea as to who you have become. So now it's time to take the new and different you into the future. Yes, I know the life you really wanted didn't happen, and I'm not minimising that. It will always be with you, but I hope you realise by now that loss and grief don't have to define you. You absolutely *can* be happy. You have freedom and flexibility in your life and you can decide how to use them.

What Do You Want?

It's time now to start living and telling a new story of your life. You've let that old sad story go, and you've spent time in between stories doing work. Now it's time to start telling a new one and to flesh out what you would like your new life and story to look like. None of us know what will happen in the future, but now is time to take it in your own hands and frame it to suit who you are and what you'd like your life to be.

In this last chapter you're going to be using everything you've learned so far and any creative flair you wish to harness so that by the end you'll have something creative to represent the future you want. If the word 'creative' brings you into a tailspin, a list is okay.

Before we do this, here's some inspiration from one of Elizabeth Gilbert's Facebook posts:

Do you know where you want to be in five years? ....

If you don't have a plan for where you're going to be in five years, then – after five years have passed – you will still be exactly where you are right now.

I know you don't want to stay the same, sad and feeling low. After all the work you've done, it's just a small push now to the finishing line. One thing is certain, time will pass. In five years do you want to have a life you love, or would you rather be in exactly the same place thinking 'I wish I'd made the effort'?

I have some questions for you to do this and before you start, here's some inspiration from the storytellers and myself.

Johanna Walker. Because I didn't have kids, I've had to work harder to give my life meaning. I've had to really radically practice self-love and self-worth, and to connect with spirit. I've worked to believe in my own worth and value – separate from what I do and whether or not I create a person. This has been a huge gift to me and in my bones I believe to other women and to the world. And it has allowed me to go after a bigger life.

It's also given me a great deal of freedom. Lots of times when I was deep in the grief I would say, 'I don't care about freedom. I want a child. I would give up all the freedom in the world for a child.' And that was maybe true, but now, when I notice the freedoms I have that my parent friends don't have – I recently had the time and resources to jump on a plane and take a two-week vacation in the south of France, to write and do my own creative work – I find myself thinking…hmm, this isn't so bad

Pamela Mahoney Tsigdinos. I was talking to a woman in New York, who said women who have children easily, who move through the typical day to day existence of being a parent don't always understand how they fit into the world because they don't always have the time to sit and contemplate it. She said for many people life is quite ordinary; they pack a lunch, they send the child off, they help them with homework, and they get up the next day and do it all over again.

Society's norm is people who pair off and have children. They can pretty well anticipate a road map of what's ahead. For those of us women who did not have the familiar or conventional routine we are forced to create our own routine, our own road map. In that sense we are in many ways living a rather extraordinary life because the world is not suited to our patterns. We have to create our own 'normal' and then adapt it to society's normal.

Many people don't realise until they retire or become an empty nester how they want to invest their time or evolve themselves; or the way they go about their day to day. We are thrust into that position unwillingly. And as a result, we are given a chance to shape our lives younger than most people. There is flexibility that presents itself and we have to decide is that luxury – an opportunity – or a constrictor. I see it as an opportunity.

Lisa Manterfield. I finished my first novel this year and I don't think I would have been able to do that with small children in the house. I know that many authors have children and manage to carve out precious creative time to write, but I don't know how they do it. Not having to worry about small humans allowed me to sink myself into the story and see the task through to completion.

Jessica Hepburn. Life is so short, and there are many, many glorious things to experience, having children is a glorious thing that I wished for my life and I will never get over not being able to carry and give birth to a baby. However, I absolutely recognise that there are other amazing experiences to have in this world and I'm grabbing them with both hands.

Swimming the channel was one of the most fulfilling things I've ever done in my life and it would probably never have happened if I'd been able to have my own child.

People often say to me 'how do you have the time and energy to do everything you do?' And the simple answer to that is, 'I don't have children'. But I also feel very grateful that my experience of not having children has made it possible for me to make a genuine difference in the world.

Helen Rebello. Freedom – being able to explore my own path as and when I want to, which means I have been able to indulge my lifelong tendency of being endlessly curious about life and always wanting to know more. I get to explore and learn and play and travel with my husband – which we could do with children, but it would be much more challenging, and I am grateful that we don't have to worry about being responsible for anyone other than ourselves when we travel to faraway places! We have financial freedom and we spend our money on things that add value to us, and I am grateful for that too.

Emily Jacob. I love sleeping. I can do the things with my business I wouldn't be able to do if I had children. I feel like I'm creating a legacy that's going to have an impact on changing the world and society in the future. And I'm helping many, many others create their full lives.

I'm still going to leave an imprint on the world, and it will be a really positive imprint. I'll be proud of on my deathbed. I wouldn't be able to do that in the same way if I had children. I use my mother energy in the community group I run and with my clients.

Rosalind Bubb. I think of myself as blessed and happy and peaceful. I'm very fortunate to be in a really happy marriage and nothing has changed that. I don't know how my life would have been if I'd had children. I see the parents around me having lots of joy, but also lots of stress. I don't have the same calls on my time and my energy that they do, and I'm a relatively free agent. I feel as if I'm able to give the energy and attention that I would have given to my children to the people that I work with, instead.

I love my job, helping anyone who's experienced miscarriage or childlessness to be happier and more peaceful. Because I use Skype and FaceTime, I can support people all around the world, and it really is fun to be in communication with women as far away as America and Australia. Many of them feel like friends. And it's such a joy, to seem them heal and recover and go on to live happier and more empowered lives.

I don't regret any of the things that have happened to me. I love my life, and I am only here now as a direct result of everything I've experienced. It really is possible to feel like this, and it's possible for *you* to feel like that, too. And you can make a start at any time, no matter how long ago all these things happened. It really *is* possible for you to be happy.

Tracey Cleantis. There are so many gifts. First off, I learned so much about myself from the infertility process. I learned how tenacious I am, how driven I am, and I didn't know that about myself before. It was present in my life but I didn't see it. It gave me that.

If I had gotten pregnant, I would have likely chosen to stay in a marriage that was not the right fit for me. It is unlikely that I would have had the time or energy for writing books, running a practice, doing speaking engagements, and supervising interns. Likely I would have been able to do some of those things, or even all of them, but not all at the same time the way I can now.

Karen Malone Wright. The gifts are my lifestyle: the freedom to spend my money, time, and energy how I choose, and to pursue my own happiness.

Christine Bishop. We decided that we would do things we wouldn't have been able to do if we had had a family, and to spend the money that we would have spent raising them on doing those things.

We both love to see new places and have new experiences so we decided to travel and see something of the world. We have visited many beautiful countries and seen things that we would never have seen if we'd had a family. We've watched the sun rise over the Ganges, visited the Taj Mahal in India, gone on safari in South Africa, and been within touching distance of elephants, lions, and rhino in their natural habitat. We've walked on the Great Wall of China and cuddled a baby Giant Panda in a conservation centre.

And we can spend quality time with our nephew and niece and spoil them rotten, then hand them back to their parents and collapse with a glass of wine in peace and quiet!

August. My husband aspires to be a full-time writer. Not having children means he can focus his spare energy on pursuing this dream.

I too love to write, and I'd love nothing more than to be able to inspire or help others through this creative pursuit. I also want to continue to travel and see the world. This is a freedom I could not have if I had children.

Enza Gandolfo. Every journey teaches us something. For me the struggle to have children was a long and painful journey but I came out of it with a sense of gratitude for what I have and the privileged life that I lead. This was the most important gift.

I know that it takes a lot of work and energy to bring up a child, and I have put my energy into other areas of my life – my writing, my teaching, my relationships. Maybe I would never have written a novel or finished a PhD…these are things I value and appreciate having had the opportunity to do.

Helen G. There is no particular plan and I still don't know how I want my future life to look or be. What I do know, however, is that as time passes I feel more strongly about being acknowledged as a childless couple. In our family-centric society we often feel invisible and that our feelings are seldom taken into consideration or acknowledged. Being part of this book and maybe being brave enough to speak out in our own social groups and community is the way to address this, perhaps. In the meantime, I can choose to be content with this life that I have now.

Louise. I have many nieces, nephews and godchildren. I indulge them and we spend time together doing fun things. They know I'll be there for them in the tough times.

Not having children has made it possible to take jobs that do not fit with the usual 9 to 5 routine. My previous job with an international charity meant I travelled from time to time in Africa, Asia, and Central America. I had never lived oversea and in 2012 I took the plunge and went to work in Malawi for two years and then in Dublin. All very interesting and challenging; and some people tell me I'm brave. To me, it's my way of leaving a legacy in the world.

I am also free to take holidays off peak and I can have more of them.

Linda Rooney. Sleeping in! Okay, so that was my automatic response, but there are in fact many positives in not having children. Choice is probably the biggest one, and something we might forget we actually have, given that many of us didn't choose not to have children. Choice comes from having the time and flexibility to live our lives in the way we want to (other issues notwithstanding, of course). Time is a huge part of that; time to be myself, to help others, to devote to my marriage and my relationships and my aging mother, to travel, to exercise, to learn new things, to write, and to keep a thoughtful, open and, I hope, generous mind.

I had the time to volunteer for an ectopic pregnancy charity, a daily commitment I almost certainly wouldn't have been able to make if I'd had children. I found volunteering to be very fulfilling, teaching me as much as I was able to teach others.

Travelling has always been much easier without children – we have had both the disposable income (that friends would spend on their children) and the time and flexibility to be able to do this.

Jill Duffin. Having returned to my career for 12 years, I found it was no longer giving me job satisfaction. When the chance to go for voluntary redundancy came up I seized it with both hands and a great big smile on my face! Friends with children off to university have been quite envious that I no longer have to work.

I feel that now is my time. It is great to make plans to do more travelling. To take up interests that have laid on the back burner for a long time. I've recently taken up playing the piano, something I have wanted to do since I was a child. I've overcome several fears such as swimming out of my depth and cycling in traffic.

NLP has taught me that no family is perfect. My reason for wanting a family was to create a childhood for my child that I thought I missed out on. I have accepted my family, particularly my mother for who she was. I was able to be a part-time carer with my other siblings for my mother in the last few years of her life. If I'd had children I would have struggled to find the time to be with her.

I was also able to mentor various graduate trainees at work and am glad to say that two of them have become good friends. Both trainees have chosen not to have children and I hope I am a good role model for them.

Liz Ashram. Of course, having children doesn't stop you doing things, but it does make things harder sometimes. I don't think I would have had the time or inclination to set up my own business if I'd have become a mother.

When I decided to go to university to study Spanish as a mature student, I never thought that one day I would be teaching it! Becoming a private tutor happened quite by accident and I'm now self-employed and teach all ages from two to adults. I also do a session in a local nursery that is fun and proving to be hugely successful and popular.

My Story: Grasping Life with Both Hands

I am now in a place where I love my life and it is more or less where I want it to be. I was really fortunate to be able to give up full-time work and spend time pursuing my own learning and development. We are also grateful that we can travel, especially to places that we wouldn't go with children and outside school holidays. That freedom and flexibility extends to other areas; we can both pursue our own interests, we can decide at the last minute to go out for the evening or the day. We know that we are very lucky to have such a fabulous group of childless friends and they inspire me every day. Some have also taken early retirement, or have decided on a career that pays less because it's also less stressful. They've also worked abroad, learned new skills, moved to a different part of the country, downsized to live in a smaller house, started a new business, done volunteer work, and so on.

Of course, none of these things are wholly the domain of the childless, and to paraphrase Pamela above, we are given the chance to shape our lives. It can either be a luxury or a constrictor. I, my friends, and the women here all saw it as an opportunity and I hope you do, too.

I am an only child, with no children and no parents, these are facts that I cannot change. I've learned to live without all that I've lost. I will always miss my parents and not being able to be a mother caused a deep wound. This used to hurt a lot and make me feel as though I was bobbing around in the sea at the mercy of the waves and currents.

Now I've done this work it no longer hurts and the scar tissue is thick and strong. The story I tell now is of finding happiness and joy and making the most of the gifts that this life brings me. I know who I am and my place in the world and I feel so much more anchored.

I intend to life my life to the fullest. What about you?

Journaling Questions

- Reflect on the stories above. Which resonated with you, which didn't, and why?

- Which qualities from the stories do you think apply to you, and which would you like to apply to you?

- Reflect on Elizabeth Gilbert's words. Where would you like to be in five years?

1. Wheel of Life

You completed your Wheel of Life in Act One and your scores in some or all of the quadrants will have changed as you've worked through the questions, so I suggest you start again. This time draw the wheel on a large piece of paper, leaving plenty of space around it. Once you've scored each segment, for each that has a score of less than ten, spend a few minutes imagining this aspect of your life if the score was ten.

Reflect on the differences between the two wheels.

Close your eyes, breathe slowly for a moment or two and drop the question into your whole body. Be still and listen for what answer comes up. You may find it best to do this over a few days, adding to it little by little and letting the thoughts and ideas permeate. By the end, I hope you will have a map of what your ideal life might look like.

2. Wheel of Me

Next do the same with your values. Take the values list you made earlier and for each, score the answer to the question 'how much am I living to my values?' one out of ten and then imagine what a score of ten would be. Use the same technique as above and take your time.

Now you have two wheels, and there may be some incompatibilities. This is perfectly normal.

3. Bringing it Together – Now Let's Time Travel

Now we're going to time travel, to imagine what you would like your life to be in the future.

I'd like you to set aside some quiet time for this; you'll need to be in a room with some space on the floor. Also have a notebook and pen close by. You may find it easiest to use the audio on my website. Take your time answering the questions, repeating the exercise a few times over a couple of weeks. Doing this will also allow ideas and options to percolate.

You could also answer the questions in your journal, or perhaps have your phone handy as you work through it and record yourself as you talk. The main thing is to be curious and open to whatever comes up.

Before you start, have the results of the 'This is Me' exercise in front of you. Now you know who the Me is that you'll be taking into the future

---

Spend a few moments reading and absorbing your two wheels.

When you're ready, stand up; walk to one end of the room with some space in front of you.

Imagine you're standing in the present. Imagine your future is a line on the floor stretching ahead of you. This is called your timeline.

Close your eyes and daydream your ideal future, the time where both your wheels are ten.

When you're ready step onto your timeline, walk as fast or as slow as you want along it until you get to that point in your future those wheels are ten, you're happy and fulfilled, living a life of purpose, meaning and connection.

Take time to savour everything. What can you see, hear and feel? What are you doing? Who is around you? Really see it, hear it, feel it, notice what's happening, absorb everything.

Adjust your mental picture so that it's even bigger, brighter, nearer, louder, feelings stronger, whatever is perfect for you.

Step beyond that point, with your life still being great, turn and look back along your timeline. Notice what you did, the steps you took to achieve this fabulous life.

As far as you can answer these questions:

- *Where am I living? What does my house look like? Who lives with me?*

- *How do I spend my days? What are my hobbies?*

- *What brings joy into my life? What am I interested in/curious about?*

- *What sort of people do I spend time with?*

- *How am I using my gifts?*

- *What and who make me happy?*

- *What have I let in to my life by letting go?*

- *What have my greatest challenges taught me?*

- *What have I learned from this work?*

  Pause for a few moments and take all this in.

Then when you're ready step off, stand next to the line at this point in your future. Take a look down your timeline and notice what you did to reach this point. What decisions did you make to get here?

Now walk back alongside your timeline to the present, as fast or as slow as you want, noticing along the way what supported you in achieving the life you want. Pay attention to what you did to make it happen. Come back to the present with the knowledge of how to achieve this life you want and how to get there.

When you get to the present, step back onto your timeline, absorb everything you learned.

What are you going to do now, tomorrow, next week and next month to get to your ideal future?

When you're ready, step off, back to now. And spend a few moments writing it all down.

You may get the best results if you do this a few times over a couple of weeks, remembering of course that nothing is set in stone. Once you have a good idea of how you'd like your life to be, get creative; make something to remind you of what you want. At the simplest, it could be a word or two to remind you, or you could do a vision board with pictures from magazines or the Internet. The important thing is to have a reminder that you can see regularly. If it helps to do so, break it down into smaller steps.

Each day ask yourself, 'What's one small step I can take this week which will take me closer to the life I want?' Then take it.

And Finally...

Thank you so much for trusting me. It has been an honour to guide you.

As I make the final tweaks before sending my manuscript to the editor, I am reflecting on just how much I've changed in the year I've been writing this book. I am not the same person who sat at this desk wondering what to write. As you've read, I've taken a wholehearted dive into the subjects of each chapter, and I can now confidently say that I am truly owning my story, showing up, and letting myself be seen. Many of my friends applaud me for my courage, but, although courage is one of my values, I don't feel that what I've done has been brave or courageous. I feel that I've got this far by letting go of expectations and taking one small step at a time.

It's not just that, though. The keys were that I trusted myself and my teachers, and I did everything with an open mind. I am always open to change, to asking for help and to learning something new about myself and about life. These, to me, have been most important.

When I started writing I was doing everything I could to avoid the pain, and now I agree wholeheartedly with this quote you read in the preface by Baal Shem Tov, *'let me fall if I must. The one I will become will catch me'*.

My falling was beautiful, because it encouraged me to do what was needed for the true Lesley to catch me. I found many gifts in my pain and the biggest gift was myself.

Now, having done the work I am a completely different person. Well maybe not *completely* different. I am now closer to being the true, authentic Lesley. The Lesley who wears bracelets and leopard skin boots and paints her nails blue. The old Lesley would never have considered any of these things, but the new me is happy to experiment and play with different looks and ideas.

I am finally comfortable in my own skin and confident when I say that *'I absolutely love my life, the adventures I'm having and I'm excited about what will happen next.'*

It is absolutely true that coming to terms with a childless life changes you. The storytellers and I have made the most of these changes to become the most beautiful we can be. By now I hope you know in your bones that you can do this too.

A Grateful Heart

A book is never written alone, and in my case it has taken an army of supporters and encouragers who I would like to acknowledge.

To my wonderful childless friends Melanie, Jill, Judy, Lisa, Eleanor, Ann, Dulcie, Hazel and Jill. Thank you for seeing me, for being there through tears and laughter, and for keeping me grounded.

To the women who have generously shared their stories, thank you. Especially to those who are not bloggers or used to sharing their story openly. I thank you for your courage and strength.

We all need people to encourage us, and especially those who hold up a 'believing mirror' to show us who and how we can be in the world. A number of beautiful women have done that for me and four in particular. So, a wholehearted thank you to:

Karen Knott, the first time we spoke you believed in me and the difference I wanted to make in the world and even when my belief has wavered, yours hasn't. You are the best supporter and cheerleader a girl could wish for. This means so much to me.

Helen Rebello for guiding me on the first gentle steps to discovering my body and myself without making it all too "woo woo" and for encouraging me every step of the way.

Melanie Mackie, for really seeing me and asking me difficult questions which encouraged me to dig deeper with my writing.

Dearest Emma Peel, because without the work we've done together this book wouldn't have happened. You knew more than I did of what I needed and in your beautiful den you've gently encouraged me to do so many things I never thought I could and you brought me home to me. I will never be the same. Thank you.

I would have given up many times if not for the endless support and encouragement of my Mastermind and Business Club ladies. Several women I've already mentioned above, so I'll now thank you Linda Anderson, Pat Duckworth, Priya Tourkow, and Stacey Chapman for seeing me and creating a safe place where I could be me.

Because it all started in Vegas, thank you Karen Anderson for encouraging me to open the box to my feelings, and supporting me all the way. Thank you also to Angie Krieger Bergen for sharing tears and laughter and for your unwavering friendship and support.

To Jeremy Lazarus for starting me on the road to discovering who I am. To Beverley Glick for introducing me to the power of story and helping to uncover mine. To Gill Sampson for making therapy a place where I felt completely at home, and for gently challenging and encouraging me. To Karen Williams for support and encouragement to get this book on the road and Sheryl Ann Andrews for those two clean language sessions that unlocked so much.

Thank you to Andrea Pennington, MD, C.Ac. for supporting me and to your team at Mark Your Mark Global, especially the designers for the beautiful cover and Carol Taylor for being gentle with the edits.

To my small and wonderfully supportive group of cheerleaders, Caroline, Melanie, Sarah, Caron, Melanie and Karen who reassured me that I was on the right track when I wasn't so sure myself.

And last and most importantly, thank you to Roger, my rock. Being with you makes me stronger.

Resources

You can read more about me, and my blog at www.LesleyPyne.co.uk

You can download a pdf of the journaling questions, listen to the visualisations and watch video interviews with many of the storytellers at www.LesleyPyne.co.uk/bookresources

More To Life is part of Fertility Network UK, the national charity for anyone who has ever experienced fertility problems. http://fertilitynetworkuk.org/

There are many websites and blogs that provide support. I've listed just the storytellers, you can find more on my website under Resources or any of these below.

Here are the storytellers, first those who provide childless support.

Pamela Mahoney Tsigdinos is a writer and women's health advocate best known for her pioneering work writing about the personal and social impact of IVF failure. Her investigative reporting and commentary has helped expose 'fertility' industry hype and profiteering. Her book, *Silent Sorority*, broke new ground exploring what it means to live involuntarily childless. Her writing has appeared in publications such as *The New York Times, WIRED, Huffington Post* and *FORTUNE.* http://www.silentsorority.com.

Lisa Manterfield is the author of *Life Without Baby: Surviving and Thriving When Motherhood Doesn't Happen* and the award-winning memoir *I'm Taking My Eggs and Going Home: How One Woman Dared to Say No to Motherhood.* She is the founder of LifeWithoutBaby.com, the online community that provides resources, community, compassion, and support to women facing a life without children. Learn more at LisaManterfield.com.

Jody Day is a British author, social entrepreneur, former Fellow in Social Innovation at Cambridge Judge Business School at Cambridge

University, and a trainee integrative psychotherapist. Passionate about helping women without children rediscover their dreams and get their groove back, she's the Founder of Gateway Women, the global friendship and support network for childless women. She is the author of *Living the Life Unexpected: 12 Weeks to Your Plan B for a Meaningful and Fulfilling Future without Children* (Bluebird/ Macmillan 2016) http://www.gateway-women.com

Jessica Hepburn is one of the UK's leading patient voices on fertility, infertility and assisted conception. She is the author of two books *The Pursuit of Motherhood* and *21 Miles: Swimming in Search of the Meaning of Motherhood.* She also writes and speaks widely in the press and media. In 2016, following her ten-year tenure as Executive Director of the Lyric Theatre Hammersmith, she founded Fertility Fest (www.fertilityfest.com) the world's first arts festival dedicated to fertility, infertility, modern families and the science of making babies. As part of this she is leading a national arts project to improve fertility education in schools. To date she has raised over £30,000 in personal fundraising challenges for families without children and children without families which so far has included running the London Marathon, swimming the English Channel and she is currently in training for one final major challenge in 2020. www.jessicahepburn.com

Tracey Cleantis is a leading expert on living your life to the fullest. Tracey's deep understanding of the field of human potential is derived from her clinical experience as a therapist, writer, and human potential activist. Passionate about helping others reach their fullest potential, Tracey helps people examine the ways they are holding themselves back and inspires people to take actions that are unique to their own goals, dreams, and talents. She has a warm, funny, and personal touch that gently guides you to where you need to go. She is a licensed marriage and family therapist who practices in Pasadena, California. Tracey is the author of *The Next Happy: Let Go of the Life You Planned and Find a New Way Forward* (Hazelden, 2015), and *An Invitation to Self-Care: Why Learning to Nurture Yourself Is the Key to the Life You've Always Wanted, 7 Principles for Abundant Living* (Hazelden/Simon & Schuster 2017) www.traceycleantis.com

Karen Malone Wright is the founding voice and chief executive of www.TheNotMom.com and The NotMom Summit, distinctive resources of news, commentary and connections for women without children by choice or by chance.

Rosalind Bubb is a therapist based in the UK, who supports women around the world who have experienced the pain of miscarriage and being childless. She is an AAMET Accredited Certified EFT Master Trainer and practitioner and a TAT Professional, and she has been supporting people since 2004. www.miscarriage-support.com – emotional care and practical tools to help you feel better and www.PeacefulByChoice.com – easing the pain of childlessness.

August is a forty-something childless seeker, busily filling those unexpected gaps with gold. In her blog she shares stories from her last two decades – to and through depression, and now on to discovery, creativity, and a new found adventurous spirit. https://fortyandeverythingafter.wordpress.com

Linda Rooney lives precariously on a fault-line in Wellington, New Zealand after stints roaming abroad as an exchange student, in the diplomatic service and, more recently, in the business world. Self-employed, she tries to find time to write, learn languages, and travel the world with her husband. On her blog, she writes using the name Mali, about her No Kidding life on No Kidding in NZ (http://nokiddinginnz.blogspot.com).

Cali Bird loves to give gentle encouragement for people to get on with their creative pursuits, alongside their regular responsibilities like having a job or caring for their family. www.gentlecreative.com

Helen Rebello has spent over a decade helping soulful women to find more meaning and magic in their life and unlock the courage to live and work on their terms. She is on a mission to empower 100,000 women worldwide to fulfil their potential so that together we contribute to a better world. She is the author of *The Magical Unfolding,* which offers a gently empowering and liberating process to unlock your inner peace, potential and purpose, and live a more magical life. www.HelenRebello.com

Johanna Walker is a public speaking coach and storytelling expert who helps entrepreneurs and people with a mission tell their stories so their audiences sit on the edge of their seats wanting more. She believes that telling the truth of our stories truly can change the world. She's the co-producer and co-host of Truth Be Told: Boulder's bi-monthly story slam, and lives in Boulder, CO. www.johannawalker.com and www.storyslamboulder.com

Emily Jacob is a rape survivor, coach, and NLP master practitioner using her skills to help guide other rape survivors to their ReConnected Life. She is a speaker, blogger, author, and editor, breaking the silence for rape survivors everywhere. She was one of the ten survivors in the feature-length Channel 5 documentary, *Raped: My Story.* She also features in the Independent video series, Life After Sexual Violence. Emily's other career spans over 20 years in marketing strategy and capability. www.reconnected.life

Enza Gandolfo is the author of two novels, *The Bridge* and *Swimming,* which explores childlessness, friendship, and art. She is also the co-author of several non-fiction books including: *Inventory: On Op Shops* with Sue Dodd and *It Keeps Me Sane: Women Craft Wellbeing* with Marty Grace. Her short stories, essays, autobiographical pieces, reviews, and articles have been published in a range of literary journals, magazines and newspapers. She is interested in the power of stories to create understanding and empathy with a particular focus on feminist and political fiction. She is an Honorary Professor in Creative Writing at Victoria University, and a founding member of the VU Feminist Research Network.

The other experts I referred to.

Emma Peel. When Emma was young she was drawn to sitting and contemplating a natural sense of peace, timelessness and spaciousness that was inherent when she stopped. She became interested in how the movement she sat within and sensed around her – be that a flowing stream or the rising sun – could also be sensed within. This interest grew into a love of the inner transformation of finding stillness and passion for studying more and eventually sharing this potential through meditation and yoga. Emma's practices focus on exploring and gathering understanding of the ways we individually move, guiding a journey that allows practice to move beyond performing and aesthetics to feeling.

Emma initially studied Ashtanga Vinyasa 200hrs in 2011 with Yoga London. A few years on, she trained with The Yoga People in Yin & Anatomy, Rocket, Tripsicore & Mandala. Emma has since furthered her Yin Yoga training with Paul and Suzee Grilley, With-Yin Yoga and Sarah Powers. She has focused her studies in Anatomy, Traditional Chinese Medicine, Five element and Meridian Theory and Chakra meditation. Emma is a registered RYT teacher with over 900 hours of study with The Yoga Alliance Professionals. Teaching with passion and love, Emma draws upon her knowledge of the energetic layers of the body, incorporating spirituality and yogic philosophy into all her classes. www.EmmaPeelYoga.co.uk

Karen Anderson is a Licensed Marriage and Family Therapist and a Licensed Alcohol and Drug Counsellor with a practice in Las Vegas.

She works with individuals, couples, families, and groups and believes the relationship between the therapist and the client is paramount for productive treatment and ultimately for healing to occur. She is also a Certified EMDR Trauma Therapist and Certified Daring Way™ Facilitator: Brené Brown Workshops; Daring Greatly, and Rising Strong. http://www.lasvegasfamilytherapy.com/

Beverley Glick is a storytelling expert and public speaking coach and a trainer with more than 35 years of experience as a journalist and editor. She is also the co-founder of The Story Party, a regular London storytelling soiree that provides a platform for ordinary people to share extraordinary stories. http://beverleyglick.com/

My business coach was **Karen Knott**. Karen works with women in their 50s and beyond to help them channel their experience, knowledge, and energy into a first-time business, which enables them to make a difference and a solid income doing what they love. She has over 20 years business experience and is a coach, a trainer and the founder of Prime Time Business. www.primetimebusiness.co.uk

I had therapy with **Gill Sampson**, a qualified, accredited UKCP Psychotherapist and Counsellor with over fifteen years' experience of helping men, women, and couples make real changes in their lives. Gill is an Integrative Psychotherapist and draws flexibly on theory and techniques from a number of different approaches to personalise clients' therapy in accordance with their explicit and implicit needs. These approaches include CBT, EMDR and mindfulness. http://www.psychotherapylondon.org.uk/

Karen Williams supported me all the way through writing. She is The Book Mentor, and she specialises in working with business owners who want to write and publish a book that they hope will build their business. https://librotas.com/

Here's a selection of books that have inspired me, some of which I have referred to.

Rising Strong, Dr Brené Brown (Random House 2015)

Daring Greatly: How the Courage to Be Vulnerable Transforms the Way We Live, Love, Parent and Lead. Dr Brené Brown, (Gotham, 2012)

The Gifts of Imperfection: Let Go of Who You Think You're Supposed to Be and Embrace Who You Are: Dr Brené Brown, (Hazeldean, 2010)

I Thought It Was Just Me (but it isn't): Making the Journey from 'What Will People Think?' to 'I Am Enough', Dr Brené Brown (Gotham 2008)

Big Magic: Creative Living Beyond Fear, Elizabeth Gilbert (Riverhead books 2015)

Self Compassion: Stop Beating Yourself Up and Leave Insecurity Behind: Kristin Neff, PhD. (Hodder & Staughton, 2011)

Broken Open: How Difficult Times can Help us Grow, Elizabeth Lesser, (Rider Books 2004)

The Artist's Way: A Course in Discovering and Recovering Your Creative Self, Julia Cameron. (Pan Books 1993)

Playing Big: Find Your Voice, Your Vision and Make Things Happen, Tara Mohr, (Hutchinson 2014)

Letting Go: The Pathway of Surrender, David R Hawking, M.D.,Ph.D. (Hay House 2012)

Better Than Before: What I Learned About Making and Breaking Habits, Gretchen Rubin (Two Roads 2015)

Year of Yes: How to Dance it Out, Stand in the Sun and Be Your Own Person, Shonda Rhimes (Simon & Schuster 2015)

Finding Your Own North Star: How to Claim The life You Were Meant to Live, Martha Beck (Random House 2001)

Love Warrior, Glennon Doyle Melton (Two Roads Books 2016)

The Book of JOY, His Holiness the Dalai Lama and Archbishop Desmond Tutu, with Douglas Abrams (Penguin Random House 2016)

Bird by Bird: Some Instructions on Writing and Life, Anne Lamott (Anchor Books 1994)

Transitions: Making sense of Life's Changes, William Bridges, (Lifelong Books 2004)

Feel the Fear and Do it Anyway, Susan Jeffers, (Vermillion, 2007)

Man's Search for Meaning, Viktor E. Frankl (Washington Square 1959)

The Happiness Project, Gretchen Rubin, (Harper Collins, 2009)

Trauma in the body

The Body Keeps the Score: Mind, Brain and Body in the Transformation of Trauma, Bessel Van Der Kolk (Penguin Random Hose 2014).

Waking The Tiger, Healing Trauma, Peter A Levine, with Ann Frederick. (North Atlantic Books 1997)

Yoga

The Complete Guide to Yin Yoga: The Philosophy and Practice of Yin Yoga, *Bernie Clark* (White Cloud Press 2011)

Yin Yoga: Principles and Practice, Paul Grilley (White Cloud Press 2012)

Grief

Grief Works: Stories of Life, Death and Surviving, Julia Samuel (Penguin Random House 2017)

Option B: Facing Adversity, Building Resilience, and Finding Joy, Sheryl Sandberg and Adam Grant (Penguin Random House 2017)

The Grief Recovery Handbook, John W James and Russell Friedmand (Harper Collins 2009)

On Grief and Grieving, Elizabeth Kubler-Ross and David Kessler (Simon & Schuster 2005)

Meditation

The Wise Heart: Buddhist Psychology for the West, Jack Kornfield (Rider books 2008)

How to Meditate: a Practical Guide to Making Friends With Your Mind, Pema Chödrön (Sounds True 2013)

The Places that Scare You: A Guide to Fearlessness, Pema Chödrön (HarperColins 2001)

I find the teachings and free meditations offered by Tara Brach to he really helpful. https://www.tarabrach.com/

You can read more about Jon Kabatt Zinn and his MBSR programme on his website https://www.mindfulnesscds.com/

I have learned a lot from the programmes offered by Sounds True, including those I referred to here, Cheri Huber, *Unconditional Self-Acceptance,* Shinzen Young, *Break Through Difficult Emotions* and Tara Brach, *Radical Self-Acceptance* and *Mindfulness Daily* (with Jack Kornfield).
https://www.soundstrue.com/store/

Story

Storycatcher: Making Sense of Our Lives through the Power and Practice of Story, Christina Baldwin (New World Library 2005)

The Secret of the Shadow: The Power of Owning Your Whole Story, Debbie Ford (Harper Collins 2002)

Do Story: How to tell your story so the world listens, Bobbette Buster (Do Book Company 2013)

NLP

NLP at Work, The Essence of Excellence, Sue Knight, (Nicholas Brealey, 2010)

Successful NLP for the Results You Want, Jeremy Lazarus, Crimson Publishing, 2010

Words that Change Minds, Shelle Rose Charvet, (Kendall/Hunt Publishing Co, USA, 1997)

About The Author

Lesley Pyne believes that it is possible to have a fulfilling life as a childless woman. She spent the first 50 plus years of her life putting everything she didn't want to feel in a box, including her grief following multiple failed fertility treatments and the loss of both parents. In the process of writing this book she dug deeply into the subjects she writes about including, grief, letting go, connecting with your body, self-acceptance and writing. She is a Neuro Linguistic Programming Master Practitioner. NLP is the study of the language of the mind, patterns of thinking and behaviour. Lesley writes openly about her challenges and how she has emerged as a different person, who is able to say confidently 'I absolutely love my life, the adventures I'm having, and I'm excited about what will happen next.' She lives in London with her husband Roger. Her website is www.LesleyPyne.co.uk

MAKE YOUR MARK GLOBAL

Get Published Share Your Message with the World

Make Your Mark Global is a branding, marketing and communications agency based in the USA and French Riviera/ Monaco. We offer publishing, content development, and promotional services to heart-based, soul-conscious authors who wish to have a lasting impact through the sharing and distribution of their transformative message. We can also help authors build a strong online media presence and platform for greater visibility.

If you'd like help writing, publishing, or promoting your book, or if you'd like to co-author a collaborative book, visit us online or call for a free consultation. Call +1 (707) 776-6310 or send an email to andrea@MakeYourMarkGlobal.com
www.MakeYourMarkGlobal.com